John E. Vigar is a professional histo
life. Although his roots are firmly witinm ine county his work takes him
to many parts of England, researching, writing and lecturing on many
aspects of architectural and social history. He appears on radio and
television from time to time. He is the author of five books, and writes
regularly in local and national journals. Mr Vigar serves on several
national Committees, notably those associated with the preservation of
medieval churches. His hobbies include cinema architecture and visiting
the seaside. He is single and lives in an historic part of the Medway
Valley.

Frontispiece
Princess Pocahontas in St George's Churchyard, Gravesend (see No 69).

Kent Curiosities

John E. Vigar

Best wishes
John E Vigar
Aylesford

THE DOVECOTE PRESS

First published in 1992 by The Dovecote Press Ltd
Stanbridge, Wimborne, Dorset BH21 4JD

ISBN 0 946159 95 5

© John E. Vigar 1992

Phototypeset in Times by The Typesetting Bureau Ltd
Wimborne, Dorset
Printed and bound in Singapore

Reprinted 1996, 1998

Contents

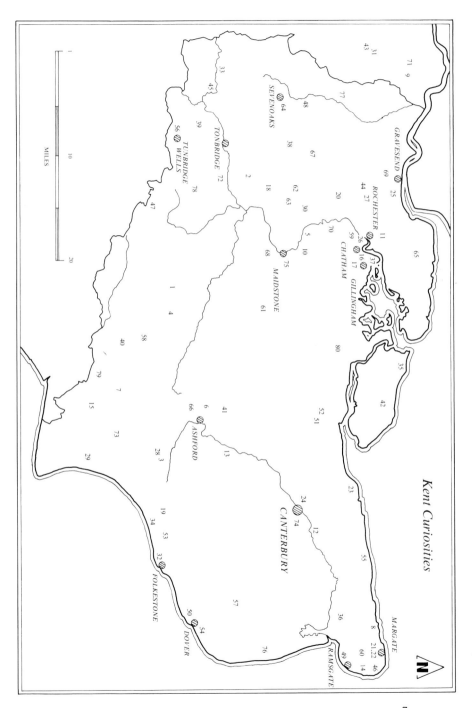

Kent Curiosities

MARGATE

RAMSGATE

FOLKESTONE

DOVER

CANTERBURY

ASHFORD

MAIDSTONE

TUNBRIDGE WELLS

TONBRIDGE

SEVENOAKS

GRAVESEND

ROCHESTER

CHATHAM

GILLINGHAM

MILES
10
20

N

7

Introduction

It is always a pleasure to be able to write a new book, for it gives one the opportunity of re-visiting places that one has not been to for a long time. Return visits are always useful things as they often show something new, or prove that one's memory of the first visit was sadly flawed. Frequently I find that my memory of somewhere visited bears a distorted view of the place in question.

Our whole appreciation of something depends on the circumstances of our visit – was it wet, were we in a hurry, was a wedding on at the church, did we talk to a local resident? In fact I often tell my students that several visits are necessary for one to gain a good insight into the history and development of an historic building, otherwise our mental images all tend to merge into one.

When looking at curiosities it is even more important to pay attention to detail – the wording of an epitaph, the construction of a folly, the topography of the locality – because the feature in question should only be taken as part of an ensemble. No building, no life story, no event, must be taken on its own. The study of local history is one of comparison and everything in history is relative; wheels within wheels.

It is essential to remember that there were never any 'good old days' – in sixty years time the 1990s will be referred to as ' the good old days'! History is about our lives today as much as about lives in the past, and when we realise this it becomes a subject of the present; to enjoy and savour.

Perhaps the stories in this book will bring a smile, or a tear. This is as it should be, for history is all about people, who had the same aspirations, hopes and fears as we have today, and I hope that you will enjoy reading about some of the more unusual aspects of Kent history as much as I have enjoyed compiling them.

John E. Vigar
Aylesford, 1992

Acknowledgments

The author would like to express his grateful thanks to the many people who have assisted in the preparation of this book, with special thanks to the following for the use of illustrations: London Borough of Bexley, Brian Slade Esq, Arthur J. Cassell Ltd, The Rt Hon The Earl of Guilford, Thanet District Council, L. A. Longhi; Bleak House Museum, Hever Castle Ltd, The Channel Tunnel Group Ltd, Arthur Percival MBE, Romney, Hythe and Dymchurch Railway, Wolfgang Heigl; Margate Shell Grotto, Chatham Historic Dockyard Trust, David Peacock Esq, The National Trust, Tunbridge Wells Borough Council, The Leeds Castle Foundation, James Loudon Esq and The Vicar and Churchwardens of Hythe Parish Church.

1 Where the Prisoners were not Well

Position: Sissinghurst Castle.
Map reference: Sheet 188; 808384
Access: Sissinghurst Castle belongs to The National Trust and is open
to the public at advertised times during the summer.

Sissinghurst Castle was built in the middle of the sixteenth century by
Sir Richard Baker as a large courtyard house, with a tall entrance
gateway. It was certainly complete by 1573 when Queen Elizabeth
I stopped there on her famous 'Progress' through the county. The
Queen only stayed there for three days, but it seems that she almost
bankrupted the family. Fifty years later the family finances suffered the
final blow – the house and estate were confiscated by Parliament
because the then owner, Sir John Baker, had supported King Charles I,
and he only reacquired the estate by paying for it. Sir John's son had
only daughters to succeed him and on his death in 1661 the estate was
split between them. This was a sure disaster – each daughter struggling
to make their part of the estate pay.
  Luckily, near the house was a natural spring to which people resorted
when ill. This had previously been a source of much annoyance to the
Bakers, who had railed it off to protect their privacy. Now, in the dying
years of the seventeenth century, they tried to capitalise on their natural
resources, and started advertising the Well as a tourist attraction,
claiming that the waters were better than those at Tunbridge Wells, and
that it was nearer to London, and moreover that Sissinghurst Castle
was available to let for the season! It was all to no avail. The wells at
Tonbridge were established on 'the circuit' of Spas towns, and there was
no need for a rival well in the locality.
  In 1756, the Government leased the house for use as a Prisoner of
War Camp for French seamen captured during what became known
as 'the Nine Years War'. Records show that between 1500 and 2000
men were imprisoned there at any one time. Conditions were appall-
ing, with large numbers of men being confined in small spaces. The
prisoners took it out on the buildings, tearing down the panelling and
starting riots. On one occasion an English soldier was killed when a
prisoner dropped a bucket on him from the top of the tower! When the
war ended in 1763 the prison closed and compensation was paid for
damages caused by the Prisoners, but this was not enough to cover even
wear and tear and by the end of the eighteenth century the house was
gradually being demolished. The only part of the castle to survive intact

was the Gatehouse.

The estate struggled on as a working farm until 1930 when Vita Sackville-West and her husband Harold Nicolson bought it and started to restore the castle and create a garden. It was no coincidence that they had picked Sissinghurst, for Vita was a direct descendant of the Baker family who had built the Castle. History, they say, always goes full circle; it certainly has at Sissinghurst.

Places of Interest in the Neighbourhood
Two's Company (Biddenden)
The Cause of the Goodwin Sands (Tenterden)
Where Ships once Sailed across the Fields (Smallhythe)

2 Mr May's Folly

Position: Hadlow village, East of Tonbridge
Map reference: Sheet 188; 634497
Access: Privately owned, but may be viewed from the adjacent churchyard.

One of the most famous Kentish landmarks, Hadlow Tower, or May's Folly, dominates the flat landscape of the Upper Medway Valley. Local legend recalls that it was built by Walter Barton May, Squire of Hadlow, in 1840 because his wife had left him! No one is quite certain if he was distressed at his wife's departure and built the tower as an aid to getting her back, or whether he was celebrating the fact she had gone! In fact it is one of these occasions when fact and fiction are somewhat confused. His wife did leave him, but it was after he'd built the tower – possibly because he'd built it!

The brick tower was based on William Beckford's famous tower at Fonthill in Wiltshire, built some forty years earlier. It is Gothic in style and was really the final stage of Mr May's house, Hadlow Court Castle which had been under construction for about fifteen years. From a distance it appears to be of stone, but this is a common nineteenth

Hadlow Tower before the demolition of the castle.

century deceit, performed by the use of a stucco known as 'Roman Cement'. This was used by builders who could not afford to use proper dressed stone, but who wanted people to think that they had. Only now, viewed at close quarters, can one see the stucco peeling off to reveal the brick underneath.

Hadlow Court Castle was demolished some years ago, but the Tower and adjacent stable blocks were retained and converted to reasonable sized houses. Access to the tower is not possible, but it can be seen from miles around and a closer inspection is possible from the adjoining churchyard where Mr May is buried in an elaborate mausoleum, itself worthy of study.

Places of Interest in the Neighbourhood
The Hartlake Bridge Disaster (Hadlow)
Margery the Martyr (Pembury)
A Little Bit of Old Italy (Mereworth)

3 Saint or Sinner?

Position: The Chapel at Court at Street, Aldington
Map reference: Sheet 189, 091352
Access: The Chapel can be seen from a public footpath.

Every so often a prominent local figure becomes part of national history. In the early sixteenth century Elizabeth Barton of Aldington became famous throughout the land. With the benefit of hindsight we are able to unravel the complex political, religious and sociological problems that led to Elizabeth being known locally as 'The Holy Maid of Kent'.

Elizabeth was born in 1506, and at a very early age was engaged as a maidservant in the household of Thomas Cobb, a steward to the Archbishop of Canterbury. The house in which she lived and worked still stands just outside the village. Lambarde's *Perambulation of Kent* published in 1576 gives the most accurate account of the curious events that led to her untimely death.

In 1525 she started to suffer from fits and trances. After she recovered her composure she was able to tell friends of events happening some distance away, and her parish priest believed that these fits were divinely inspired visions. Encouraged by him Elizabeth began to tell her stories throughout the village and week by week hundreds of pilgrims came to see her at a little chapel at Court at Street just outside Aldington.

Eventually she was admitted to a convent in Canterbury, where the church, finding itself in financial difficulties through the work of Henry VIII, manipulated Elizabeth into speaking out against Henry's marital situation. Henry could have caused trouble for Elizabeth there and then, but Archbishop Warham of Canterbury stood up for her. Unfortunately Warham died in 1532 and Elizabeth lost her only influential ally. Cromwell ordered that she be tried for treason and in April 1534 she was hanged at Tyburn.

Today the chapel at Court at Street is in an advanced state of decay, but many visitors still find their way to this picturesque spot to reflect on the wide ranging implications of Elizabeth's power and popular support.

Places of Interest in the Neighbourhood
The Aldington Gang (Aldington)
Where a Dastardly Plot was Hatched (Saltwood)

14

Elizabeth Barton's Martyrdom – a theatrical representation!

4 Two's Company

Position: Biddenden lies between Headcorn and Tenterden.
Map reference: Sheet 189;851384
Access: The Maid's effigies are on the village green.

Eliza and Mary Chulkhurst were England's first recorded Siamese Twins, born in the parish of Biddenden in about AD1100.These poor sisters were joined at the waist and the shoulders, and must have been looked upon as either a judgement from God, or as freaks. They lived together for over thirty years – a remarkable age when one considers the period – but one of the sisters (no one is really sure which one) died, and her sister refused to be separated from the corpse, dying a few hours later.

The Chulkhurst twins must have been fairly wealthy, for they left a parcel of land to provide an income to perpetuate a charity in the village. The charity distributed cheese, bread and ale to the poor each Easter, and the lands which provided the income became known as the 'Bread and Cheese Lands'.

Each Easter the charity still operates, although now the recipients receive a hard inedible biscuit, upon which is stamped a picture of the twins. The distribution is quite a popular event and provides a good photo opportunity as it takes place out of doors.

On the village green is a wooden painted effigy of the twins, showing them in Elizabethan Dresses – the twelfth century not being remembered as a period of glamorous costumes!

Places of Interest in the Neighbourhood
Where the Prisoners were not Well (Sissinghurst)
The Cause of the Goodwin Sands (Tenterden)
Where Ships once Sailed across the Fields (Smallhythe)

The Biddenden Maids sign on the Village Green.

5 A Machine for the Drowned

Position: Aylesford village is to the NW of Maidstone
Map reference: Sheet 188; 729591
Access: The resuscitator is on permanent loan to Maidstone Museum
where it may be inspected on request.

The village of Aylesford owes its very existence to the River Medway
which runs through it. It was here, in AD455, that the English nation
was formed when the army of Hengist and Horsa met that of King
Vortigern at the ford.

In the nineteenth century a lawyer, John Adams, witnessed an horrific
accident at Aylesford when a wagon fell into the river, drowning its
occupants. He felt so helpless that he left a sum of money in his will to
commission a 'Drowned Man Resuscitator' to be given to the village.

The eminent inventor, John Read, who was responsible for both the
stomach pump and round oast house, was given the commission and his
apparatus was presented to the village in 1840. It consists, somewhat
improbably, of a pair of beautifully crafted bellows, with a selection of
nozzles, tubes and other attachments. All fit into a charming Mahogany
box inscribed with the name of the donor.

The machine was kept in the George Inn next to the river in Aylesford
– as much for the benefit of those coming out of the bar late at night and
falling in as for any other eventuality. But it was never used. There
were no instructions with it, which may have put would be users off
experimenting on drowning persons. After the closure of the Inn, it was
decided to place the Resuscitator on loan with Maidstone Museum.

John Read, it's inventor, lived in Kent at Horsmonden where he is
commemorated in the church by a marble bust.

Places of Interest in the Neighbourhood
The Sphinx of the West (Boxley)
Was Lady de Leybourne Heartless? (Leybourne)
The Fire on the Heath (Penenden Heath)

6 Some Unique Volunteers

Position: Godinton Park, Ashford
Map reference: Sheet 189; 982438
Access: Godinton Park House is open to the public at advertised times during the summer.

Godinton Park is one of the most interesting small manor houses in the county, and is famed nationwide for its wealth of carved wooden panelling. The house was built in the fifteenth century, but substantially remodelled on several subsequent occasions, most notably in the early seventeenth century by Captain Nicholas Toke.

Captain Toke was an ardent Royalist, and amongst the many examples of the woodcarvers art which he introduced to the house, those to be found in the Great Chamber on the first floor are of supreme importance as they depict Kentish volunteers engaged in Pike and Musket drill.

There are dozens of little men each showing a different position in their drill, all carved in high relief near the ceiling. Local tradition says that they were carved by itinerant Hugenot craftsmen, and it is a shame that no records survive of the names of the craftsmen involved. Kentish Volunteers were raised at several times in the county's history, more especially at the time of religious persecution in the sixteenth century when Mary I took a dislike to the county on account of its high proportion of extreme Protestants, and it would have been with this religious intolerance in mind that Nicholas Toke might have commissioned a Hugenot to record scenes that probably took place in the parkland surrounding Godinton House.

Places of Interest in the Neighbourhood
For Priests or Pests? (Great Chart)
The Incognito King (Eastwell)
An Eventful Life (Wye)

7 The Largest Ditch in England

Position: Appledore
Map reference: Sheet 189; 958292
Access: The canal runs from Hythe to Rye, but may be seen to
advantage at the village of Appledore.

The Royal Military Canal is a unique defensive ditch constructed in
1803 on the orders of William Pitt, who feared that Napoleon might
invade England via Romney Marsh. It is 23 miles in length, and forms
an effective boundary between the low marshland and the rising ground
of the Weald of Kent.

   The Canal was really a second line of defence, as Martello Towers had
been built on the coastline to shoot at troops as they landed – but if the
towers failed in their duty, and troops made it across the Marsh, the
Canal would have stopped their progress. In any case English troops
could have been brought down to resist the invasion in the time it took

The Royal Military Canal near Bonnington.

the French to cross the Marsh.

A further advantage of the canal was that it could be used to flood Romney Marsh, further hampering the enemy. A complicated system of commands was established to cover all eventualities, but a false alarm whilst the Canal was being built nearly resulted in the flooding of the Marsh forever. No-one had thought how it could be restored should a flooding prove necessary!

As it was, the Canal was obsolete before it was completed. Money to pay for it had only been supplied in dribs and drabs, and there were too few troops to patrol it anyway. In times of invasion cardboard cut-outs of soldiers would have been placed along the banks to make it look fully manned!

Today the Canal is used to drain the Romney Marshes, and by countless fishermen.

Places of Interest in the Neighbourhood
The Pagan Altar in a Christian Church (Stone in Oxney)
The Shocked Steeple (Brookland)
A Room with a View (Romney Marsh)

8 A Campanologist's Dream

Position: Quex Park, Birchington
Map reference: Sheet 179; 311681
Access: The Tower (not open) stands in the grounds of Quex Park Museum which is open to the public at advertised times during the season.

Quex Park is best known today for the Powell-Cotton Museum housed in purpose built galleries attached to Quex House. Yet the history of this site is just as interesting as the collections which are open to the public.

In the early nineteenth century the estate was owned by John Powell Powell, a much respected figure in Kentish Society. He was appointed as High Sheriff for the county, on which occasion the pub in the village changed its name from the 'New Inn' to 'The Powell Arms'. Within his park at Quex he built two towers. The earliest is a plain round structure that gave him a view out to sea, and allowed him to signal passing ships using flags raised from the top of the tower. He would sit up there for hours on end looking out for a familiar ship, whereupon he would fire a cannon to attract the captain's attention, and then start his correspondence!

Soon after building the round tower he embarked upon a much more grandiose scheme for building a bell tower. John Powell Powell was a gifted campanologist and composed many ringing methods. The joy of bell ringing is that the more bells you have the more complicated methods you can compose. Few churches in Kent have more than eight bells and John Powell Powell wanted twelve. About a quarter of a mile from his house he built a tower to hold the peal and, as if that wasn't enough, he erected a huge cast iron spire on the top that can still be seen for miles around.

Less the bell ringers get exhausted in their endeavours to ring his compositions he provided four small rooms at the base of the tower as refreshment, or beer, rooms.

Today the bells are still rung regularly by a Society of Change Ringers, and no doubt John Powell Powell would be pleased to know that his tower, built in about 1815 and named after the Battle of Waterloo, still gives pleasure nearly two hundred years later.

Places of Interest in the Neighbourhood
The Strange Story of St Mildred (Minster in Thanet)
A Royal Playground (Margate)

9 Where the Rake made Little Progress

Position: Hall Place. Bexley
Map reference: Sheet 177; 501743
Access: Hall Place is open to the public at advertised times throughout the year.

Hall Place is a part Tudor, part Jacobean Country House that stands uneasily between the A2 dual carriageway and the urban sprawl of outer London. The present house dates in the main from the sixteenth century, and was built by Sir John Champneys, a former Lord Mayor of London. At that time Bexley would have been a little village a day's journey from the capital. Champneys had made his money through

Hall Place, Bexley.

trading, and following the Dissolution of the Monasteries had been able to purchase a large quantity of building stone from abandoned monastic foundations in the area, which he used to enlarge his new house. In many parts of the building re-used stonework can be seen, most of it dating from the thirteenth and fourteenth centuries.

In 1772 the ownership of Hall Place passed to one of the most famous rakes in eighteenth century England, Sir Francis Dashwood of Buckinghamshire. Sir Francis had run the famous Hell-Fire Club in a ruined abbey on the banks of the Thames, and had he realised the monastic connections at Hall Place he would probably have used it in his rituals, but as it was it just appeared to be an old, draughty and inconvenient house, and he decided not to use it personally. The Dashwoods let it to tenant farmers until the twentieth century when it was eventually sold to the local council who now run it as a museum and local studies centre.

Places of Interest in the Neighbourhood
The Lost View (Bexleyheath)
Where the Eagle Landed (Chislehurst)
Tunnels of Dubious Origin (Chislehurst)

The White Horse Stone.

10 The Sphinx of the West

Position: The White Horse Stone, Boxley
Map reference: Sheet 188; 753603
Access: The stone stands just to the north of the Pilgrims Way, behind a petrol station on the A229 Bluebell Hill.

The Medway Valley between Wrotham and Boxley was settled at a very early date, and there are the remains of many prehistoric burial chambers to be found on the valley slopes. Two, Kits Coty House at Aylesford, and the Coldrum Stones at Trottiscliffe are well known, but there are others, including the White Horse Stone, that deserve study.

In the nineteenth century there were two White Horse Stones, standing quite near each other, but one was destroyed to facilitate easier ploughing. They took their name from the White Horse Standard that was raised here at the Battle of Aylesford in AD455.

Hengist and Horsa, the Jutes, used the white horse as their emblem when fighting against Vortigern of Kent. When Vortigern was defeated in battle the emblem was adopted as that of the Kings of Kent, and later as the emblem of the county.

It is interesting to recall that the stone chosen by Hengist and Horsa as their base camp had been placed there by previous occupants of the site several thousand years earlier! It probably formed part of a large burial chamber which has been destroyed. A limited excavation in the nineteenth century showed that the stone had been artificially sited on a bed of small pebbles, and was not left there by a trick of nature.

In the nineteenth century an increased awareness of things ancient resulted in many people describing the stone in books and journals, and the most fanciful wrote that it reminded them of the Sphinx! Whilst in some lights a head might be imagined on the end of the stone, it certainly could not compete in size, being only a few feet high.

Places of Interest in the Neighbourhood
A Trip to the Underworld (Maidstone)
The Fire on the Heath (Penenden Heath)
A Machine for the Drowned (Aylesford)

11 The Wet Railway

Position: Strood and Higham Canal Tunnel
Map reference: Sheet 178 ;740698
Access: By taking a train journey from Strood to Gravesend. Either end
of the tunnel may be viewed from a distance, most easily at Strood
Station.

History is always a story of continual change and adaptation, but few
of those who built the tunnel between Strood and Higham can have
dreamed that one day it would be used to carry trains!

When it was opened in 1824 the tunnel carried the Thames and Medway Canal, built to link the two major Kent rivers for the benefit of
those carrying their cargoes by water. Until the construction of the
Canal the journey linking Gravesend with Strood by water took nearly
fifty miles around the coast, but with the Canal the trip was reduced by
almost four-fifths.

Work started on digging the canal in 1800, but money soon ran out,
and it wasn't until 1818 that progress was made to start the tunnel,
which was to be over 4,000 yards long.

As the tunnel was to carry sea going boats it had to be much larger
than other canal tunnels, and consequently cost a great deal more. In
1830 it was decided to breach the tunnel about a third of the way along
its length in order to let in some daylight and create a passing place.
Today the traveller by train cannot fail to notice the short period of
fresh air between two lengths of tunnel.

The Canal was never a success. Although it was always busy the
revenues received hardly covered the running expenses, let alone repay-
ment of the initial capital. In 1844 the canal company decided to
increase their revenue by laying a single track railway along the tow-
path, and through the tunnel. The first train ran in February of the
following year. Local rumours tell that the congregation in nearby
Frindsbury Church ran for their lives with the vibrations from beneath
their feet, and that the first train through lost its funnel which hit the
top of the tunnel!

After a while the South Eastern Railway took over the line, filled in
the canal completely and laid a double track in the tunnel, keeping the
canal open only from Gravesend to Higham. The Thames and Medway
Canal Tunnel saw shipping for only about 20 years, and has seen rail
traffic ever since. Few travellers today would realise that 150 years
ago they would have been travelling by boat through this extraordi-

The remains of the Canal at Higham Railway Station.

nary feat of engineering. A Trust has been formed to restore and re-open what remains of the Canal between Gravesend and Higham for pleasure purposes, and their admirable work can be seen from the railway.

Places of Interest in the Neighbourhood
The City Centre Alpine Retreat (Rochester)
Where Shells Reign Supreme (Cooling)
Where did Dickens spend his Honeymoon? (Chalk)

12 The Forgotten Port

Position: Fordwich stands to the NE of Canterbury
Map reference: Sheet 189; 182598
Access: The Court Hall is open to the public at advertised times during the summer.

The many visitors to Canterbury may be forgiven for omitting a visit to the tiny village of Fordwich from their itinerary. Yet, it if hadn't been for Fordwich the development of Canterbury would have been much slower. Both places lie on the River Stour, but only Fordwich was able to cope with river traffic, being that much nearer the sea.

From early times Fordwich acted as the port for Canterbury, and the Caen stone used to build the Cathedral passed through it. During the latter part of the Middle Ages, when Fordwich was a 'limb' of the Cinque Port of Sandwich, the river started to silt up to such an extent that the town declined rapidly. No amount of dredging at Sandwich could prevent the river becoming virtually useless as a means of carrying goods, but even with its raison-d'etre gone the town kept its status until the end of the nineteenth century.

Today one can visit the picturesque Court Hall, built during the early sixteenth century when the Port was all but finished. It is timber framed, the gaps between the timbers being filled with brick nogging. The Court Hall was also used as a prison and a damp prisoner's cell may still be seen. At the end of the building, abutting the River, is Crane House, used to unload shipping at the highest point of navigation. It had a second purpose as well, for old hags who had been taken to Court for gossiping were strapped into a ducking stool attached to the end of the crane and given a good soaking in the river! After their ordeal they were sent upstairs to a small room at the end of the Court Hall set aside for them to change into dry clothes. The ducking stool is now preserved in the Museum housed in the Court Hall.

Fordwich lost its status as a town in 1886, but remains a place of great charm, its historical importance not quite forgotten.

Places of Interest in the Neighbourhood
The Head was under the Bed (Canterbury)
Dane John's Dungeon (Canterbury)
Southern England's First Passenger Railway (Whitstable)

13 An Eventful Life

Position: Olantigh stands to the N of the village of Wye
Map reference: Sheet 189; 061485
Access: The grounds of Olantigh are occasionally open to the public,
but the statue of Mr Erle Drax may be seen from the road.

The nineteenth century produced many larger then life figures who ran
their country estates with great aplomb. With its position close to London Kent attracted the great and famous who chose to live here rather
than in some far flung part of the country.

One to make the others pale into insignificance was Mr JSW Erle-
Drax, who lived at Olantigh, a house in the village of Wye. His ances-
tors had lived in the area for some time, but he had married a wealthy
heiress from Dorset, bringing money and prestige back to the Kent
estate.

As a Major in the East Kent Volunteers Mr Erle-Drax had achieved
some distinction, and served as Member of Parliament for Wareham in

JSW Erle-Drax Statue at Olantigh.

Dorset. With such credentials he was able to indulge his eccentricities without any official reprobation, but it is certain that his tenants had plenty to say behing his back!

Mr Erle-Drax was a great horseman, and used to keep a pack of hounds at Olantigh. His hunt had its own private colours of orange and black, and terrified the villagers who occasionally had to stop the trains when the hunt jumped the level crossing gates on the edge of the village.

About twenty years before his death, Mr Erle Drax had a rehearsal of his funeral, following the whole procedure through from a discreet distance. He had even made a dummy of himself and had it placed in the coffin. Unfortunately, the estate workers who had to carry the coffin up the drive decided that the weight was too great and jettisoned the dummy behind a yew hedge. Mr Erle Drax was less than pleased, believing that the same fate might happen to him on his actual funeral day! It is said that he even kept the coffin propped up behind his bedroom door, in case he popped off unexpectedly!

He could see that national heroes like the Duke of Wellington were having statues erected to their memory in London, and thought it was about time someone commemorated him. He sent out tickets inviting people to subscribe to a statue, but little money came forth. Not wishing to be outdone he paid for it himself. Then came the crunch. Where was the statue to be erected? He rather fancied Whitehall or Trafalgar Square, but the authorities thought otherwise and in the end a special railway wagon had to be constructed to transport the statue to Wye where Mr Erle-Drax had it erected outside the main door of his house where it remained for some thirty years until it was moved by his nephew and heir to a more discreet position away from the house. Another monumental work which Mr Erle-Drax erected at Wye, a huge fountain purchased at the Great Exhibition of 1851, was also removed and may now be seen in Victoria Park, Ashford.

Visitors to historic houses will be interested to know that Olantigh was one of the first to be opened to the fee paying public. Mr Erle-Drax had such a wonderful art collection that he issued tickets so that the public could inspect his galleries. Unfortunately the house was gutted by fire in 1903, and many items destroyed. Soon afterwards the house was sold, and whilst the family is still represented in the area the connection with Olantigh and the 'Mad Major' is now in the past.

Places of Interest in the Neighbourhood
The Incognito King (Eastwell)
Some Unique Volunteers (Ashford)
For Priests or Pests? (Great Chart)

14 The Empty Chair in an Airy Nest

Position: Bleak House, Broadstairs
Map reference: Sheet 179; 400680
Access: Bleak House is a private museum and is open to the public at
advertised times most of the year.

High on the clifftop at Broadstairs stands Bleak House, the seaside
home of Charles Dickens, the nineteenth century novelist. During his
time it was known as 'Fort House', but it was later renamed in honour
of one of Dickens novels. Dickens loved Broadstairs and its people –
the position overlooking the bustling harbour, and the seclusion when
he needed it. *David Copperfield* was written here.

It was not just in his novels that Dickens described the house. Many
letters survive to show what it was like. One, written to an American
friend captures the spirit of the place:

"This is a little fishing place, intensely quiet, built on a cliffe, whereon
our house stands; the sea rolling and dashing under the windows. Seven
miles out are the Goodwin Sands whence floating lights perpetually
wink after dark, as if they were carrying on intrigues with the servants.
Under the cliff are rare sands, where all the children assemble every
morning and throw up impossible fortifications, which the sea throws
down again at high water. Old gentlemen and ancient ladies flirt after
their own manner in two reading rooms and on a great many scattered

Bleak House, Broadstairs.

seats in the open air. Other old gentlemen look all day through telescopes and never see anything."

Today the house, which the author often called 'an airy nest' contains many Dickens momentoes, the most important of which is undoubtedly the 'Empty Chair'. At the time of his death Dickens was staying at his other Kent house, Gad's Hill at Higham. The Society artist Sir Luke Fildes was due to do an engraving of Dickens, but the author died whilst Sir Luke was on his journey to Higham. Not wishing to waste the journey Fildes drew Dicken's study at Gad's Hill, showing his desk and chair as they had been left on the day of his death. The subsequent engraving summed up all the Victorians felt about Death, and was a best seller.

After his death, all Dicken's effects were sold, and the chair can now be seen in Bleak House. Everything points to this being the actual chair – but just to add to the mystery there are two other 'Empty Chairs', one in London, the other in America!

Places of Interest in the Neighbourhood
The Kentish Sampson (St Peters in Thanet)
The Created History House (Kingsgate)
The Eighth Wonder of the World (Margate)

The detached steeple at Brookland Parish Church.

15 The Shocked Steeple

Position: St Augustine's Church, Brookland
Map reference: Sheet 189; 989258
Access: The church stands in the centre of the village.

Brookland church has a detached steeple, built completely in wood, in three stages.

As with many unexplained aspects of local history it has given rise to many legends. One is that the spire originally stood on the church, but blew off! Another says that it flew off in a state of shock when a confirmed old bachelor married an elderly spinster!

In reality, the soft marsh ground in the area could not have supported a tower and spire – especially one containing bells. So a bell cage was erected in the churchyard to take them. The structure can be dated by examining the joints which show a date of about AD 1260, which is contemporary with the stone-built church. In the fifteenth century a change took place in bell ringing which meant that taller bell frames were required, and the structure was heightened to its present size. To protect the bells, and the ringers, the whole structure was then clad in weatherboarding, to give its present 'candle-snuffer' appearance.

On top of the spire is an unusual eighteenth century weathervane depicting a dragon with a forked tongue!

Places of Interest in the Neighbourhood
A Room with a View (Romney Marsh)
Where the Wheels Run Smoothly (New Romney)
The Largest Ditch in England (Appledore)

16 The Extravagant Prophet

Position: Gillingham, Kent
Map reference: Sheet 178; 775670
Access: Jezreel Road leads off Rainham Road, Gillingham. Gillingham Library holds a large archive on the sect.

At the top of Chatham Hill the name of a small road is now the only reminder of a once legendary building and its nineteenth century founder. Jezreel Road stands on the approximate site of Jezreels Tower, built in 1885 by James Jershom Jezreel, leader of an extraordinary religious sect.

In the early nineteenth century there lived a prophet called Joanna Southcott. After her death many sects were formed devoted to her teachings, one of which was called The New House of Israel. They had churches all over England, one of which was here in Gillingham. In 1863 the local church leader, John Wroe, died leaving them without a figurehead. It was about this time that a soldier, James White, joined the branch and gained the confidences of the members to such an extent that they saw his arrival as a sign that he was to be their appointed leader. To reinforce their decision he changed his name to James Jershom Jezreel, a name he had found in Hosea Chapter 1. Unfortunately the New House of Israel's National Headquarters in Ashton under Lyne refused to recognise Jezreel as the new leader of the Gillingham Church, but not to be outdone Jezreel formed a breakaway church called 'The New and Latter House of Israel'. To join one had to sell all possessions, and donate one tenth of all income to the sect. As they grew more powerful the members bought local shops and kept money in the group by encouraging members only to spend their money in sect shops. By this means a large amount of money was accumulated. Jezreel bought himself a large house in which meetings took place, but eventually this was not large enough. He travelled abroad and calculated that over 1,400 people were members of his sect.

It was obvious that they needed a suitable base, and at the top of Chatham Hill Jezreel started to build a temple. It was a brick and concrete tower which measured 83 feet on each of its four sides. It was to have been 100 feet tall, with a central atrium in which revolving floors would have accommodated the never ending stream of Jezreelites who would have flocked here to attend Jezreel's sermons.

Unfortunately money quickly ran out. There were allegations that Jezreel had appropriated large sums for his own use, and even worse, that he had committed many serious offences, including child abuse. His popularity plummetted and just two months after work on the tower had begun, he died at the age of about 45. His wife, who then adopted the name 'Queen Esther' continued her husband's work, but died herself at the age of 28 three years later. The sect struggled on, but without the dominant figureheads of James and Esther could not possibly survive.

The tower was left unfinished – a gaunt shell that was a landmark to many a traveller on the main London road. There it remained until 1960 when it was finally demolished. It had been so well constructed that the work took fourteen months to complete. The rubble was used to build the foundations of the M2 motorway bridge which was then under construction.

Places of Interest in the Neighbourhood
An Englishman Abroad (Gillingham)
One of Kent's Longest Buildings (Chatham)
Poor William of Perth (Rochester)

17 An Englishman Abroad

Position: Gillingham
Map reference: Sheet 178; 785668
Access: The clock tower stands on the main A2 between Chatham and Rainham.

Will Adams was born in Gillingham in 1564. Like many young men of his period he was greatly influenced by the close proximity of Chatham Dockyard, and decided to seek his fortune at sea. After an apprenticeship spent in London he went to the Barbary Coast where his job was to service English war ships with provisions.

His great ambition was to open up new trading routes to India and China and in 1598 he joined a Dutch trading expedition to the Far East. Of the three ships that started out in the expedition, only Adams's ship

The Adams Memorial Clock Tower.

successfully completed the journey by landing in Japan in April 1600. At this time Portugal had sole trading rights with Japan, and the Portugese persuaded the Shogun to imprison Adams and his crew, because they viewed him as a threat to their monopoly, but the Shogun saw the possibilities of having further western trading partners and decided to do a deal with Adams.

The Shogun spared Adam's life on condition that he remain in Japan, building ships for the Japanese. Under his influence the Dutch East India Company established permanent trading links with Japan, with Adams working as a type of Ambassador. He was on good terms with the Shogun who rewarded him with many privileges, allowing him to marry a Japanese girl – even though he still had a wife living in England.

After Adams's death in 1620 he was buried in Japan, and all trading links with the West were broken. It was not to be for another 250 years that another Englishman set foot in Japan. Adam's story has recently been brought to a wide audience with the book and television series of 'Shogun' and he is rightly remembered as an early Ambassador between the two countries.

In 1934 a clock tower was erected to Adam's memory in a prominent position in Gillingham to show the continued links between the two countries. It is a marvellous monument to the town's most famous son.

Places of Interest in the Neighbourhood
The Extravagant Prophet (Gillingham)
One of Kent's Longest Buildings (Chatham)
The City Centre Alpine Retreat (Rochester)

18 A Little Bit of Old Italy

Position: The village of Mereworth lies between Maidstone &
Tonbridge on the A26.
Map reference: Sheet 188; 668533
Access: Mereworth Castle is not open to the public, but the
contemporary church is open daily.

Travellers along the A26 are often seen to glance down the drive of
Mereworth Castle with a sense of awe and amazement. For this 'castle'
is one of the finest Palladian Villas in England.

It was built in about 1720 by Colen Campbell for the Hon.John Fane
(later 7th Earl of Westmorland). Campbell had travelled in Europe and
had seen Palladio's Villa Rotonda in Vicenza. Mereworth Castle, which
was to replace a rambling medieval house, was designed as far as possible as a copy of this Italian masterpiece. John Fane was a young and
wealthy patron who wanted a house that would not only be an ideal
summer retreat, but which would be a showpiece in its own right. It
was a fairly small building, with just two state bedrooms, two drawing
rooms, a salon and a hall on the ground floor, with limited guest accommodation on the floor above.

When, in 1736, John Fane inherited the earldom he realised that the
house was not large enough for his new status, and two pavilions were
added as free standing structures to the north of the main block, form-
ing a pleasing tripartite ensemble. Today the setting has matured and is
dominated by gigantic Cedars of Lebanon.

One of the curious features of the house is the adaptation of the
Italian model to suit the cool winters in Kent. Fireplaces were provided
in all rooms, but this caused a problem as they all required flues and
chimneys which would detract from the pure symmetry of the exterior.
Campbell cleverly incorporated flues into the linings of the Dome, and
constructed 24 chimneys in the Cupola. He was so proud of this design
that he frequently wrote that 'unless one sees the chimneys smoking one
would not know of their existence'.

Places of Interest in the Neighbourhood
The Queer Quintain (Offham)
Where a Saint was Startled (West Malling)
Mr May's Folly (Hadlow)

19 Where a Dastardly Plot was Hatched

Position: Saltwood Castle lies to the north of Hythe.
Map reference: Sheet 189; 163359
Access: Saltwood Castle is open to groups by written appointment only.

Of the many medieval castles in Kent, none are as evocative as that to be found at Saltwood. Its wall-walk is one of the few that survive almost intact, and the Keep is still very much a family home.

From the early eleventh century Saltwood was traditionally held by the church, but after the Norman Conquest it seems to have been appropriated by Barons close to the King. It had the reputation of being one of the strongest castles in the region, and in the twelfth century was the home of Henry d'Essex, Constable of All England.

In the middle of the twelfth century the Archbishop of Canterbury, Thomas a Becket, petitioned the King to restore Saltwood to its former position as an ecclesiastical palace, and the King took it from Henry d'Essex and gave it instead to one of his ruffian Barons, Ranulf de Broc.

It was during de Broc's occupation that Saltwood came into national history, for it was here on December 28th 1170, that the four knights who were to murder Becket at Canterbury the following day met to plan their deed.

They used Saltwood for three reasons. Firstly, it was the home of one of Henry II's most loyal barons. Secondly, it was near enough to Canterbury to be within a few hours ride. Thirdly, it was ideally placed near the coast – the Knights had travelled over from Normandy the previous day.

How far de Broc was involved in Becket's murder is unclear, but it is his house that has come down in history as being the scene of the final discussions before the knights rode to Canterbury.

Most of the present Castle was built by a later Archbishop, William Courtenay, but the curtain walls are certainly those known to de Broc in the twelfth century.

Places of Interest in the Neighbourhood
The Disinterred Residents of Hythe (Hythe)
A Tunnel under the Channel (Folkestone)
Saint or Sinner? (Aldington)

20 The Lost Village

Position: Dode village is near present day Luddesdown.
Map reference: Sheet 188; 669638
Access: The church may be viewed from the road.

Until the mid fourteenth century there was a village called Dode, which stood in a narrow valley on top of the North Downs. It was a small farming community, probably dependent upon the grazing for sheep that existed on this chalky downland at that time.

In the summer of 1349 the Black Death reached Kent from its passage across southern England, and this part of the county was badly hit.

At Dode it seems the entire population was destroyed. In 1367 the Bishop of Rochester wrote to the effect that no-one had lived there, or attended church there for over 15 years, and that it was not possible to keep the church open. In a brave effort to maintain a religious presence in the area he joined the parish of Dode to that of Paddlesworth a mile away, and hoped that the population would some day return. It never did.

Paddlesworth, too, had been badly hit by the Black Death, although people continued to live there until 1678 when its church was finally closed. By that stage Dode church had been a ruin for nearly three hundred years, and any hope of the area being repopulated had long been abandoned.

In the nineteenth century renewed interest in antiquarian matters led to Dode becoming something of a tourist attraction. People came to clamour over the foundations of the medieval houses, to see the roof-less church and throw stones down the fern-lined village well. One of these visitors, George Matthews Arnold, purchased the ruins of Dode church in 1901 and restored the church to something of its medieval appearance.

Today, some nine hundred years after it was first built, Dode church and its well are all that remains of the once thriving farming community. It is in an area like this that history can be seen to be a very fragile thing. Links like this must be preserved if future generations are to be able to enjoy the seclusion of this delightful valley.

Places of Interest in the Neighbourhood
The Murder at Dadd's Hole (Cobham)
Where a Deserter was Recaptured (Wrotham)
Was Lady de Leybourne Heartless? (Leybourne)

21 A Royal Playground

Position: The Theatre Royal, Margate
Map reference: Sheet 179; 355708
Access: The Theatre presents professional touring shows throughout
the year.

Margate can rightly claim to be Kent's oldest seaside resort. Early
visitors to the coast came by boat from London, rather than risk the
notoriously poor road system. Margate was about as far as they could
comfortably go from the capital- the other resorts around the headland
were just too far away. So Margate developed before the rest.

There had been a small fishing port there, but by the 1760s the village
was being converted into a town 'of noble resort'. Whilst the visitors
bathed in, and drank, the seawater, they wanted their lodgings to be in
genteel positions away from the sea spray and smells of the fishing
boats, and squares of houses were built on the hill above.

It wasn't long before travelling players from Canterbury came to

Margate's Theatre Royal.

entertain the visitors – often in the back rooms or yards of public houses. There were also one or two temporary Playhouses, but there were many squabbles between companies of players trying to attract the limited audience. The only solution to the problem was to obtain a patent for the town, giving one man the monopoly on holding theatrical performances. In the summer of 1786 a Royal Patent was issued by George III, and a purpose built Theatre Royal was erected, opening for business on June 27th 1787.

It was a rectangular theatre, capable of holding 700 people, and often full to capacity. Yet as the resort grew, so other attractions opened, including the Assembly Rooms and Tivoli Gardens, and the Theatre Royal fell on hard times. By the mid nineteenth century there were other diversions for the visitor, and despite being brought up to date and re-fitted, the Theatre Royal found it a struggle to survive. After a couple of fires and complete closure on more than one occasion the theatre has been restored, and continued recent investment has ensured that it is now well established on the professional circuit.

Not only is it a charming theatre retaining its 18th and 19th century character, it is also the second oldest theatre in England that is still in use – only Bristol's Theatre Royal being older.

Places of Interest in the Neighbourhood
The Eighth Wonder of the World (Margate)
The Kentish Sampson (St Peters in Thanet)
A Campanologist's Dream (Birchington)

22 The Eighth Wonder of the World

Position: The Shell Grotto, Grotto Hill, Margate
Map reference: Sheet 179; 359700
Access: The Grotto is open to the public at advertised times during the summer.

Far away from the hustle and bustle of Margate seafront lies a most extraordinary structure known throughout the locality as 'The Shell Grotto'. It was discovered in 1835 when the proprietor of a small school, Mr Newlove, put his foot hard down on a spade and the ground gave way to reveal a well-like hole. Mr Newlove sent for his son Joshua who was unceremoniously lowered into the hole clutching a candle. He came back talking of passages, shells and altars. His father immediately purchased the land from its owner and then set about opening the grotto to the public.

After cutting a new entrance Mr Newlove penned a few lines of welcome which were placed over the entrance:

> Enter; the scene that greets you here
> No common scrutiny demands:
> These walls, though perfect they appear,
> Were fashioned not by modern hands.
> The sea, long centuries ago
> Cast forth from its mysterious cells
> The stores here ranged; a goodly show
> Of beautiful and glittering shells.
> These by ingenious hands were wrought
> In accurate and close array,
> And eager hands, I doubt not, sought
> The Grotto of an ancient day.
> Beneath the shrouding earth concealed
> Long was it suffered to remain
> Till accident its site revealed
> And drew it to the world again.
> Gaze on these shells, so aptly placed
> In graceful, well proportioned lines:
> Mark well the harmony and taste
> Shown in the various quaint designs.

The grotto was opened to the public in the summer of 1837. Ever since there have been literally hundreds of theories as to its origin. These range from 'definitely Roman' to 'built by Mr Newlove to make money'. The writer Marie Corelli (inventor of the name Thelma) des-

Interior of the Shell Grotto.

cribed it as the eighth wonder of the world! Whilst that might be going a little too far it must be admitted that this is one of the most unusual sites in Kent.

The Grotto consists of a winding passage leading to a rectangular room. The walls and ceilings are covered with thousands of sea shells representing flowers, stars, and fertility symbols.

General opinion today is that it was built in the latter half of the eighteenth century at a time when such structures were fashionable, and that it was soon abandoned and forgotten, only to be discovered thirty years later.

Places of Interest in the Neighbourhood
A Royal Playground (Margate)
A Campanologist's Dream (Birchington)
The Kentish Sampson (St Peters in Thanet)

23 Southern England's First Passenger Railway

Position: The line ran from Whitstable to Canterbury
Map reference: Sheet 179; 116660
Access: Parts of the line may still be traced on the OS Map, especially at Clowes Wood and either side of Tyler Hill.

Unless one knows the history of East Kent, and its special industrial development, one would never guess that the oldest passenger railway in Southern England ran between Canterbury and Whitstable.

The line came into being to replace the two other methods of linking the towns – road and water. By road was quite a short distance, but along costly turnpikes. By water meant a long journey around the Thanet coastline and up the Stour, which required unloading the boats at Fordwich. This route was becoming more difficult owing to the silting up of the estuary at Sandwich.

The goods being transported included Iron Pyrites, or Copperas as it was known locally, which was used in the tanning process. Canterbury has long been a centre for tanning, and St Mildreds Tannery still exists within the City Walls.

In 1825 an Act of Parliament for 'making and maintaining a railway or tram road from the sea shore at Whitstable in the county of Kent, to or near the City of Canterbury in the said county' was passed, and work started on its construction.

The main problem was that the gradients were so steep that the traction had to be provided by a series of stationary steam engines, as well as by a steam locomotive. The original locomotive, Invicta, is now preserved in the Canterbury Heritage Centre.

The railway was opened in May 1830 to much celebration. Return trips to Whitstable were offered, and souvenirs sold. The Cathedral bells were rung and a new era dawned. Yet the dream never came true. The forty minute journey was fine for those who could afford it, but those people who thought that goods from London would now be cheaper in Canterbury were disappointed as the railway company charged high rates for loading and unloading. There were ten return trips each day, and from 1834 season tickets were available.

The early carriages were all open, and the journey, especially through the 800 yard long Tyler Hill Tunnel, was not comfortable. All the trains were mixed passenger and freight. With these factors against it the line struggled until 1853 when it was finally purchased by the South Eastern Railway. By this stage better locomotives had been introduced and the stationary engines had been abandoned.

In the twentieth century the line became popular with holidaymakers, especially those making Sunday afternoon trips to the Coast, and it was they who christened it the 'Crab and Winkle' line. Outside the holiday period the line relied on freight traffic, and as this declined so did their revenues. Finally, in 1952 British Rail decided to close the line and it was dismantled.

Places of Interest in the Neighbourhood
The Church with Two Enemies (Reculver)
The Sorry Tale of Thomas Arden (Faversham)
The Head was under the Bed (Canterbury)

The Roper Gateway, Canterbury.

24 The Head was under the Bed

Position: The Roper Gateway, St Dunstans Street, Canterbury
Map reference: Sheet 179; 143583
Access: The gateway may be viewed from the street.

The red brick Roper Gateway, recently restored, is all that remains of Place House, the former home of the Roper family. The architecture of the Gateway is pure Tudor, with a four-centered arch holding double doors. Above the doors are crow stepped gables – the up to date fashion of the time. Here and there the red bricks are relieved by a diaper pattern of black bricks, and brushed brickwork lozenges.

It was in a house behind this gateway that Margaret Roper, daughter of Sir Thomas More, Henry VIII's Lord Chancellor, lived with her husband William. In 1535 More was beheaded at Tower Hill, and his head placed on London Bridge. At dead of night his daughter Margaret hired two men to help recover her father's head, and honour.

One climbed onto the bridge and grabbed the head from the end of its pike. The other rowed Margaret underneath the bridge and at the right moment the head was dropped into her lap. She took it back to Kent, where it was placed in a box of rose petals which she kept under her bed.

A few years later the head was interred in the church of St Dunstan, which stands almost opposite the Roper Gateway, where a chapel founded by the Ropers had been rebuilt during Sir Thomas More's lifetime. A much later memorial inside the church commemorates the burial of the head in the family vault.

Places of Interest in the Neighbourhood
Southern England's First Passenger Railway (Whitstable)
Dane John's Dungeon (Canterbury)
The Forgotten Port (Fordwich)

25 Where did Dickens spend his Honeymoon?

Position: The village of Chalk lies between Strood and Gravesend
Map reference: Sheet 177; 677310
Access: The Honeymoon Cottages stand in the High Street.

Charles Dickens spent his honeymoon at Chalk. That is fact. But there are three possible claimants to the exact property.

The one that every local knows is Craddock's Cottage, an extremely picturesque weather boarded house in the High Street. A bust of Dickens over the front door is all the proof required for most visitors that this was the honeymoon cottage. However, this modern interpretation does not tie in with more contemporary accounts. In a book published just 20 years after his death Dickens is recorded as having stayed at 'a large comfortable farm house which fronts the Dover road at a corner of a lane leading to the vicarage'. Craddocks Cottage certainly does not fit this description, and only one house, The Manor House, does.

The third claimant, Mrs Nash's weatherboarded cottage nearby only became involved in the controversy because it was confused with Mrs Craddocks, and is the least likely of the three.

Much of Dicken's *Great Expectations* was based on this part of Kent, and Joe Gargary's Forge may be seen further down the High Street. The prison hulks moored in the Thames below Chalk, from which the prisoners often escaped were also included in the book, and would have been clearly visible from the village. At the Parish Church visitors can still see the 'comical old monk carved in stone' over the West Doorway, to which Dickens always doffed his hat.

Places of Interest in the Neighbourhood
A Red Indian Princess (Gravesend)
The Wet Railway (Strood)
Lord Darnley's White Elephant (Cobham)

One of these two cottages is where Dickens spent his honeymoon: (top) *Craddock Cottage,* (bottom) *The Manor House.*

26 The City Centre Alpine Retreat

Position: Dicken's Chalet, Rochester
Map reference: Sheet 178; 746684
Access: The Chalet stands in Public Gardens behind the Dickens Centre in Eastgate. The exterior only may be seen.

In 1856 Charles Dickens purchased Gad's Hill Place at Higham, between Strood and Gravesend, a house that he had admired since a boy. He was to live there for the rest of his life.

One day news came that 58 crates addressed to him had arrived at Higham Railway Station. On closer inspection these proved to be a 'Do it Yourself' Swiss Chalet sent as a present by his friend Charles Fechter.

Dickens eagerly set to work erecting the Chalet in a little piece of shrubbery that he had planted on the opposite side of the main road to Gad's Hill Place, where he furnished it as a Study. However, he found it rather inconvenient having to cross the road several times a day, and eventually dug a foot tunnel to connect the front lawn of Gad's Hill with the shrubbery opposite. The tunnel still exists.

Inside the Chalet he installed mirrors to reflect the changing lights and moods, and to make his little room seem part of the treetops. He described it soon after its arrival:

'It will really be a pretty thing, and in the summer (supposing it is not to be blown away in the spring), the upper room will make a charming study. It is much higher than we supposed.'

After Dicken's death in 1870 the contents of Gad's Hill were sold, and the Chalet transferred to London where it became a tourist attraction. His family decided it should be brought back to Kent where it was erected in the grounds of Cobham Hall. As a wooden structure it took a lot of maintenance, and by the late 1950s was in a sorry state. Through the initiatives of both the Rochester City Council and the Dickens Fellowship the Chalet was saved and erected in its present position behind the Charles Dickens Centre in the centre of the City – a little bit of Switzerland that is now very much part of Rochester's heritage.

Places of Interest in the Neighbourhood
Poor William of Perth (Rochester)
One of Kent's Longest Buildings (Chatham)
The Wet Railway (Strood)

27 The Murder at Dadd's Hole

Position: Dadd's Hole, Cobham Park near Gravesend
Map reference: Sheet 178; 689685
Access: Dadd's Hole is on a public footpath that runs through the Park
of Cobham Hall.

Today there is a growing appreciation of nineteenth century art, and
one of the most popular artists is Richard Dadd, born in Chatham in
1817. His father was an apothecary, obtaining much of his business
from Chatham Dockyard and its ever-changing population. Richard
was educated at King's School in Rochester where he discovered his
talent for painting and sketching.

In 1842 Sir Thomas Phillips embarked on an ambitious journey to the
Middle East and took Richard Dadd with him to record what they saw.
It was whilst on this expedition that Richard began writing back to
friends saying that he sometimes doubted his own sanity. Later writers
have suggested that over exposure to the sun caused this 'madness', but
it now seems likely that there was some genetic defect in the family, as
several of his brothers and sisters suffered similarly.

On his return from the expedition in the summer of 1843 his condition
worsened. He thought he was being pursued by the Devil in disguise,
and drew horrific pictures of his friends. In an attempt to calm him
down his father decided to take him for a holiday in Kent, to visit
Cobham Park where he had sketched as a child.

The two men booked into an inn in Cobham at the end of August and
went for a walk in the Park where the poor father was stabbed to death
by Richard using a knife and razor. His body was found in a shallow depression known to this day as 'Dadd's Hole'. After the murder
Richard cleaned himself up and fled the country, but was soon arrested
after trying to repeat the exercise in France! He was brought back to
England where he was admitted to Bedlam in the summer of 1844. He
wasn't expected to live long – but in fact he spent the next 42 years in
various institutions, including Broadmoor. Throughout his imprison-
ment he painted with great gusto, and it is these later paintings that are
so collected today.

Richard Dadd died in January 1886 at the age of 69.

Places of Interest in the Neighbourhood
Lord Darnley's White Elephant (Cobham)
The Lost Village (Dode)

28 The Aldington Gang

Position: Aldington village stands on the edge of Romney Marsh
Map reference: Sheet 189; 063366
Access: The Walnut Tree public house is in the centre of the village, The Bourne Tap is at Aldington Frith, and Aldington Knoll stands on the B2067.

The village of Aldington was for long the centre of the Kentish Smuggling trade.

The leader of the smugglers was George Ransley, who came from a family notorious for its law breakers. There had been burglars, highwaymen, smugglers and assailants in the family. In 1820 the Aldington Gang, or 'Blues' as they are now known, was formed to cover the whole area of Romney Marsh. Their first recorded 'run' was at Sandgate in November that year, which involved over 200 smugglers unloading a boat from Boulogne. One of the reasons that the gang was so successful is that there were always more smugglers than excisemen, and whilst the excisemen usually put up a good fight their action was little deterrent.

Ransley lived at the Bourne Tap, a house he built for himself at Aldington, and which was used as an illegal drinking house for his smuggled goods. He had little regard for the Walnut Tree Inn in Aldington village, which was in direct competition with him. Some nights Ransley would ride through the village, breaking the windows of the Inn as he sped through. Over a period of months this led to his loss of status amongst the ordinary villagers, who had previously turned a blind eye to the 'goings on'.

In July 1826 the gang took part in a 'run' at Dover in which an exciseman was killed. A reward of £500 was offered for information leading to the arrest of the culprit. This was too much for the folk of Aldington who reported the names of all the gang members to the authorities. In the autumn raids were made on the houses of the accused and nineteen men arrested, including Ransley. In January 1827 they appeared at Maidstone Assizes, and were ordered to be transported to Van Diemen's Land (Tasmania). After several years good conduct Ransley was given a pardon, but not allowed to return to England. His wife and children travelled to Australia where their descendants still live.

Places of Interest in the Neighbourhood
Saint or Sinner? (Aldington)

29 Where the Wheels Run Smoothly

Position: Romney Hythe and Dymchurch Railway
Map reference: Sheet 189; 075249
Access: Regular trains run at advertised times throughout the summer.

The Romney, Hythe and Dymchurch Railway is the World's Smallest
Passenger railway, operating a regular service for the benefit of school-
children throughout the year, with a much enlarged service for tourists
during the summer months.

It was the brainchild of two men – Captain J.E.P. Howey and Count
Louis Zborowski – who decided to open a miniature railway in the
1920s. Their first choice of sites, in Somerset and Sussex did not

The Romney, Hythe and Dymchurch Railway.

materialise, but in 1925 they set out to build on the flat levels of Romney Marsh. The Light Railway Order for the first eight and a half miles between Hythe and New Romney was granted in 1926 and the following year it opened, with a narrow guage of 15 inches. Two years later the extension to Dungeness was opened, bringing the total length of line to nearly 14 miles.

Throughout the 1930s the railway was extremely popular, bringing holidaymakers to their camps on the Marsh at Dymchurch and St Marys Bay. During the war it was taken over by the Military and was extensively used to transport the secret PLUTO pipeline.

Places of Interest in the Neighbourhood
The Shocked Steeple (Brookland)
A Room with a View (Romney Marsh)
The Largest Ditch in England (Appledore)

30 Was Lady de Leybourne Heartless?

Position: Leybourne Parish Church, near West Malling
Map reference: Sheet 188; 689589
Access: The church is open at times of services.

During the Middle Ages people who died abroad were not usually brought back for burial in their home church. Instead, it was common practice to dissect the body and to bring back small pieces such as the heart, brain and bowels, that could be encased in lead. Throughout England there are about 30 instances of this having happened, nearly all in the thirteenth century when the Crusades were at their height.

In 1271 Prince Edward embarked on the final crusade to the Holy Land. Accompanying him was Sir Roger de Leybourne, a former High Sheriff of Kent and advisor to the Prince. Poor Sir Roger hadn't been abroad long before he was killed. His body was dissected and his heart brought back to Kent for burial in the parish church which stands next to Leybourne Castle. There it was interred under a small stone casket in a double monument. In 1286 Edward I visited Leybourne to visit the tomb of his friend and advisor, and together with his wife, Queen Eleanor, gave two iron crowns to the church as a token of respect. Those crowns are still to be seen in the church today.

When the church was being restored in the last century the Victorians opened up the monument to see which of Sir Roger's bits were contained therein! Of the two caskets, the first to be opened carried the inscription 'The heart of Roger de Leybourne'. In this type of monument elsewhere the other casket had always contained the wife's heart – but here at Leybourne it was found to be empty and had never been used! Historians puzzled over this for some time, but then discovered that Lady de Leybourne had married again, and that she must have been buried elsewhere! There is only one other thirteenth century 'Heart Shrine' in Kent, at Brabourne near Ashford.

Places of Interest in the Neighbourhood
The Queer Quintain (Offham)
Where a Saint was Startled (West Malling)
A Tale of Two Stones (River Medway)

31 Where the Eagle Landed

Position: Chislehurst Village
Map reference: Sheet 177; 455701
Access: Royal Parade stands near St Nicholas' Church. The Cross
Memorial may be seen on the Common. Camden Place is now a Golf
Club and is not open to the public.

In September 1870 the French Emperor, Napoleon III surrendered to
the German Army at Sedan. His wife, Empress Eugenie, and his son the
Prince Imperial, fled to England where they took accommodation at
Hastings. Within a few days the Empress had heard that a house at
Chislehurst, Camden Place, was available for occupation, and on September 20th that year they moved to Chislehurst, to be joined there the
following spring by the Emperor himself.

They knew the area, and the house, through a rather complicated
story which involved a settlement on an illegitimate child born to
a woman called Elizabeth Howard, who afterwards became the
sweetheart of Napoleon III, before his marriage to the Empress
Eugenie. It seems that the trustee for this settlement was Nathaniel
Strode of Chislehurst – the owner of Camden Place, and that Strode
had for some time been busy preparing the house to receive the
Emperor.

The Royal family were popular residents in the village. They brought
prosperity to the area, and many noble visitors, including Queen
Victoria, who was a frequent guest. Royal Parade, the small row of
shops near the Common still has the Imperial Eagle proudly displayed.
However,there were some minor irritations. The French sent spies to
the village to make sure that the family were not making plans to return
from exile, and stories are still told of spies taking over the windmill to
be able to get a good view of Camden Place.

The Emperor died in January 1873 and was buried at St Mary's
Roman Catholic Church where his widow erected a mausoleum to his
memory.

His son, the Prince Imperial joined the British Army and died in 1879
fighting the Zulus at Itelezi. His funeral at Chislehurst was an outstanding affair, with the Prince of Wales being a pall-bearer, together with
other Royals from across Europe. There were over 100,000 people assembled on the Common. The following year the people of Chislehurst
erected a cross on the Common to his memory.

The Empress wished to build a second mausoleum at St Mary's

Prince Imperial Memorial, Chislehurst Common.

Church, but there was no more space, and she was forced to move to Hampshire where she founded an Abbey at Farnborough, and with this completed the bodies of her husband and son were exhumed and moved there.

Places of Interest in the Neighbourhood
Tunnels of Dubious Origin (Chislehurst)
The Lost View (Bexleyheath)
Where the Rake made Little Progress (Bexley)

32 Memorial to a Physician of Note

Position: Folkestone Town Centre
Map reference: Sheet 189; 225355
Access: The statue stands on the corner of Clifton Gardens.

The statue of William Harvey at Folkestone immediately tells you why he should be remembered. In his left hand he is shown holding a deer's heart, whilst his right holds his own. William Harvey is the man who discovered the circulation of the blood.

He was born in Folkestone in 1578, and was educated at King's School, Canterbury. After Cambridge he travelled to Padua where he studied anatomy, and on his return to England was elected a Fellow of the College of Physicians.

Harvey was a physician to James I, and because of his position was always cautious about broadcasting his discoveries until he was certain of them. Eventually, in 1628, he felt comfortable enough to publish the results of his experiments, but many of his colleagues ridiculed his ideas.

One of the problems people had in accepting his theory on the heart was that Harvey had been wrong in the past. He had often lectured on the superior position of the male of the species, using a talking parrot as an example. It was only after the parrot's death that it was discovered that it had been female, thus throwing his theory completely.

Harvey also embarked on some most unusual campaigns, which included sun bathing naked on the flat roof of his London house – at a time when the slightest touch of colour on one's face was ridiculed!

Later he was appointed Surgeon to Charles I and accompanied him on his campaigns, including attending on the King at the Battle of Edgehill in 1642. As a Royalist supporter his house in Lambeth was burnt by the Parliamentarians, destroying the results of much research.

When Harvey died in 1657 he was buried in the church of Hempstead, Essex, having long given up his Kent connections. He had given his only landholding in the county, a farm on Romney Marsh, to the Royal College of Surgeons.

Places of Interest in the Neighbourhood
A Tunnel under the Channel (Folkestone)
The Disinterred Residents of Hythe (Hythe)
Where a Dastardly Plot was Hatched (Saltwood)

The statue of William Harvey at Folkestone.

33 An American's Tudor Village

Position: Hever Castle near Edenbridge
Map reference: Sheet 188; 478452
Access: Hever Castle is open to the public at advertised times throughout the summer.

Hever Castle is a picturesque moated castle, dating in the main from the fourteenth century when Sir John de Cobham was given licence to crenellate his property. It later passed to the Bullen family, and was the childhood home of Anne Bullen, or Boleyn, who became Henry VIII's second wife. After the Bullen family's fall from favour the Castle passed to the Crown, and Henry gave it to his fourth wife, Anne of Cleeves. After her death it was sold to a yeoman family and became less of a stately home and more of a country farmhouse.

By the end of the nineteenth century it was little more than a ruin and in 1903 it was purchased by William Waldorf Astor. Astor was a very wealthy American with a fortune based upon trading, newspapers and

The 'Tudor Village' at Hever Castle.

racehorses. He had become disenchanted with America and had moved to England, buying Cliveden House in Buckinghamshire in 1893.

On a trip to Kent in 1901 he fell in love with Hever and two years later purchased the Castle and six hundred acres of land. He embarked on a huge programme of rebuilding and enlargement of the castle and its environs. The main problem was the size of the castle – far too small for the lavish standard of entertaining he had introduced at Cliveden. But as the Castle was moated it could not be enlarged.

The answer was to build a 'Tudor Village' behind the castle to act as new guest accommodation, and to join it with the original building with a covered bridge. Without a doubt the new ensemble is a complete success. Each part looks as if it was designed by a different person over several decades of the sixteenth and seventeenth centuries. In fact the village was built in one go, in 1904, with each 'separate' building in reality being a series of passages and luxurious suites. In all over 100 rooms were added.

The River Eden had been diverted to create an area large enough to build the 'Tudor Village' and was dammed to form a huge ornamental lake at the far end of the formal gardens which Astor planned to use to show off his vast collection of statuary.

The present owners of Hever Castle have cleverly adapted the 'Tudor Village' for corporate use, and this provides an income to ensure the continued maintenance of the Castle.

Places of Interest in the Neighbourhood
A Little Bit of the East comes West (Chiddingstone)
An Inventor Extraordinaire (Southborough)
Home of 'Disgusted' (Tunbridge Wells)

34 The Disinterred Residents of Hythe

Position: St Leonards Parish Church, Hythe
Map reference: Sheet 189; 161351
Access: The Crypt is open to the public at advertised times during the summer months.

On the continent it is the custom to preserve bones in an ossuary, but very few churches in England have this sort of structure. The bones at Hythe are housed in a processional passage built beneath the east end of the parish church. As the processions during the middle ages became less common, so the passage was given over to the store of unwanted bones.

There are few things we can say for certain about these bones, but we do know that they have been shown to the public for nearly two hundred years, for in 1816 Richard Chamberlain was allowed 'the sum of £1 in addition to his present salary of £4 a year and the privilege of showing the bones'. Many people have eagerly come up with solutions as to why the bones are here at all. Were they those of bodies washed up along the coastline? Perhaps they were the many plague victims who died in successive waves of the Black Death?

Like most fanciful theories the reality is rather less exciting. In the middle ages burials could only take place in churchyards – there were no cemeteries. As town centre churchyards became full they were systematically cleared of burials, leaving the ground free to be used again. Often the old bones were thrown out, or used as fertiliser, but here at Hythe the larger bones, and skulls, were saved and placed in the convenient passageway under the church.

This systematic clearance is one reason why churchyards rarely have monuments dating from before the seventeenth century, all burials being commemorated by a single communal cross.

The crypt at Hythe is arranged with shelves of skulls along one side, and a pile of larger bones along the other. They have all been dated to the medieval period, and include the skulls of people who suffered from bone diseases. One victim at least had had an operation to remove pressure on the brain, and some may have met violent deaths. A few are much smaller than others and these are not children's skulls, but come from the heads of very small people. In the middle ages we were all on average four inches shorter than we are today, so this is one positive indication as to the age of the skulls.

Throughout the Middle Ages Hythe was a bustling Cinque Port, but its importance, and population, declined as the sea retreated. Today the town is a mile from the sea.

Places of Interest in the Neighbourhood
Where a Dastardly Plot was Hatched (Saltwood)
A Tunnel under the Channel (Folkestone)
Memorial to a Physician of Note (Folkestone)

Hythe Crypt contains hundreds of old skulls.

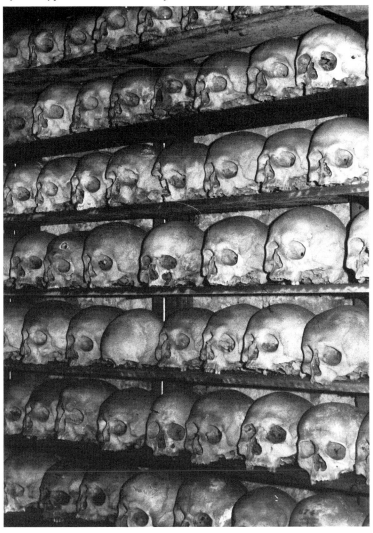

35 The Ship on the Shore

Position: Minster, Isle of Sheppey
Map reference: Sheet 178; 936749
Access: The Ship on the Shore Inn stands on the beach road to the East
of Sheerness.

The Ship on the Shore is one of the most unusual buildings on the Isle
of Sheppey. Islands are always interesting places for the historian to
study because they always had an insular and unique development.In
the same way that seaside towns have their own type of architecture, so
islands have their own characteristic buildings. Many of them have
suffered a shortage of building materials over the years and one can find
all sorts of bits and pieces being used to 'mend and make do'. But few
can compete with the Ship on the Shore.

No-one is quite sure when it was built, but it seems to date to the
middle of the nineteenth century, when the growth of the cement trade
led to an increase in coastal shipping from the North Kent chalk
quarries.

At some point a ship carrying cement powder sank in the Thames
Estuary between Sheerness and Minster on Sea. When the salvage
vessels went to the wreck they discovered that the cement had hardened
in the barrels.

The resourceful people of Sheppey salvaged the barrels, which were
dragged ashore. The wooden parts were broken off and possibly used as
firewood, whilst the hardened barrel shapes were used to build a small
building. The gaps in the walls were filled with flint stones, pieces of
brick and tile, and all sorts of other rubbish. It is quite possible that this
little building was constructed as a net-house for the local fishermen, or
as a cattle shelter.

Next to the strange building stands a small public house called 'The
Ship on the Shore', although whether it predates the little building or
not is unclear. People flocked here at the turn of the last century to see
the curious structure, and small cards were printed for the benefit of
the customers. Today, it seems, few people care too much about this
isolated oddity.

Places of Interest in the Neighbourhood
The Legend of Grey Dolphin (Eastchurch)
Off like a Rocket! (Milton Regis)
An Englishman Abroad (Gillingham)

36 The Strange Story of St Mildred

Position: The Village of Minster stands to the West of Ramsgate
Map reference: Sheet 179; 313645
Access: Minster Abbey is open to the public at advertised times.

There are a handful of churches in Kent dedicated to St Mildred, one of the county's own Saints.

St Mildred's mother, Domneva, was the founder and first Abbess of Minster Abbey, in the Isle of Thanet, founded in 669AD. Mildred was sent to France for her education and whilst there had a miraculous escape from death in an oven, having been thrown into it by a jealous teacher. On arrival back in Kent she put her foot on a rock in Pegwell Bay that has been known as 'St Mildred's Rock' ever since. She took over from her Mother as second Abbess of Minster until her death and her body was buried beneath the High Altar of the Abbey Church.

In the ninth century Viking raiders sailed up the Wantsum Channel and sacked the town of Minster, burning the Abbey to the ground. In 1027 King Canute granted Minster Abbey to the monks of St Augustines Abbey in Canterbury, and in 1032, despite much local opposition, it was decided to remove St Mildred's Relics to Canterbury where they were enshrined near the tomb of her great-great grandfather, Ethelbert,

The tranquil gardens of Minster Abbey.

the first Christian King of Kent.

The former Abbey at Minster became a farm and a magnificent Parish Church was built nearby in about 1150. After the Dissolution of the Monasteries in the sixteenth century the old Abbey was sold and became a Manor House, but in 1937 nuns were able to return to their former home, and the community was refounded. The Benedictine Order has been re-established at this site of early Christianity, and an excavation in the lawn of the Abbey has discovered the site of St Mildred's Shrine.

Places of Interest in the Neighbourhood
A Campanologist's Dream (Birchington)
The Kentish Sampson (St Peters in Thanet)
The World's Largest Public Air Raid Shelter (Ramsgate)

The interior of The Ropery, Chatham Historic Dockyard.

37 One of Kent's Longest Buildings

Position: Chatham Dockyard lies to the North of the town
Map reference: Sheet 178; 759691
Access: The Dockyard is open to the public at advertised times
throughout the summer.

Chatham Dockyard was already a favourite anchorage in the sixteenth
century, with Henry VIII ordering that his ships should over-winter in
the Medway Estuary. During the reign of Queen Elizabeth I the area
became established as a Dockyard, with shipbuilding being carried on
as well as other routine maintenance work.

The history of the Dockyard is tied up with many events of national
history, and is famous as being the Dockyard where the *Victory* was
launched in 1800.

Following its closure in the 1980s the Dockyard has been turned into
a working Heritage Centre, with many of its fine eighteenth century
buildings being restored and reoccupied.

By far the most interesting building is the Ropery, built in 1785. The
ground floor is still used for making ropes, on machinery installed in
1806. The building itself is 1,140 feet long. Above the manufactory were
stores for hemp and finished rope.

There is no doubt that the Ropery is one of the longest buildings in
Kent – four times longer than nearby Rochester Cathedral.

Places of Interest in the Neighbourhood
The City Centre Alpine Retreat (Rochester)
The Extravagent Prophet (Gillingham)
An Englishman Abroad (Gillingham)

38 A Needlewoman of Note

Position: Ightham, near Sevenoaks
Map reference: Sheet 188; 584535
Access: Ightham Church is in the village centre. Ightham Mote at Ivy Hatch is open to the public at advertised times throughout the summer.

In the parish church at Ightham are two remarkable monuments. The first depicts two men resting on their elbows, Sir William Selby and his nephew, another Sir William, both of whom lived in the early seventeenth century.

The elder Sir William bought the medieval moated house known as Ightham Mote in 1591 and left it to his nephew, the second man on the monument. This second Sir William was a loyal servant of James I, and when James came down from Scotland to take the throne of England William handed him the keys of Berwick upon Tweed, and received a Knighthood on the spot.

Sir William married Dorothy Bonham, and her monument may be seen on the wall near that to her husband. She was an excellent needlewoman, as her inscription testifies:

Ightham Mote, former home of Dorothy Selby.

68

She was a Dorcas
Whose curious Needle turned th'abused Stage
Of this leud World into the golden Age:
Whose pen of steel and silken Inck enrolled
The Acts of Jonah in Records of Gold;
Whose Arte disclosd that plot, which had it taken;
Rome had tryumphed & Britans walls had shaken;
She was
In heart, a Lydia; and in tongue, a Hanna,
In Zeale a Ruth; in Wedlock, a Susanna.
Prudently Simple, providently Wary;
To th'world a Martha: and to Heaven a Mary.'

In the nineteenth century it was thought that this inscription recorded Dorothy's part in the discovery of the Gunpowder Plot, but in fact it only records that she made a needlework picture of that event in history. Behind her effigy, which was carved by the Master Mason to the Crown, Edward Marshall, are representations of her two needlework pictures.

Dame Dorothy died in 1641, having survived her husband for four years. Her house, Ightham Mote is now in the care of the National Trust.

Places of Interest in the Neighbourhood
Where a Deserter was Recaptured (Wrotham)
A Little Bit of Old Italy (Mereworth)
Lord Sackville's Birdhouse (Sevenoaks)

39 An Inventor Extraordinaire

Position: David Salomon's House, Southborough
Map reference: Sheet 188; 568417
Access: The display rooms are open to the public at advertised times
during the week.

Just outside the town of Southborough stands a unique monument to
one of the nineteenth century's outstanding scientists. The Salomons
family, who had originated in Holland, moved from their house at
Groombridge to nearby Southborough in the early part of the nineteenth century. Sir David Lionel Salomons (Sir David Salomons the
younger) who lived from 1851 to 1925 is the most remarkable member
of the family. He was a prominent member of the scientific world – at a
time when discoveries and breakthroughs were a part of everyday life,
and served as Vice-President of the Institution of Electrical Engineers.
The entire house was equipped for electricity from 1882.

During his time at Southborough he greatly enlarged the house,
adding a Tower and Science Theatre. It is the latter which is of supreme
importance, having remained almost untouched since Sir David's time.
The theatre was fully equipped for scientific demonstrations, slide
shows, lectures and concerts. Blackout and lighting facilities were
remotely controlled, and were the most up to date for their period. In
1914 a large Welte Philharmonic organ was installed – the only one to
remain in its original position.

Apart from his scientific experiments indoors, Sir David was a pioneer
of motor transport. He owned 62 different cars, and founded the Self
Propelled Traffic Association in 1895, which later became the RAC. He
was also the organiser of the first Motor Show in this country.

Sir David's daughter bequeathed the house to the 'people of Kent' and
it is now used as a training centre for the Regional Health Authority.
Two rooms are open to the public, and there are displays about Sir
David and his work.

The David Salomons Society is undertaking a programme of restoration and conservation in both the house and theatre, and it is hoped
that more public events will be held in due course.

Places of Interest in the Neighbourhood
Home of 'Disgusted' (Tunbridge Wells)
A Little Bit of the East comes West (Chiddingstone)
Margery the Martyr (Pembury)

40 Where Ships once Sailed across the Fields

Position: Smallhythe lies to the SW of Tenterden
Map reference: Sheet 189; 893300
Access: Smallhythe Place is owned by the National Trust and is open to the public at advertised times during the summer.

Most visitors to the tiny village of Smallhythe visit it to see the timber framed house that was the home of the actress Dame Ellen Terry in the early part of this century. It is only when they read the guidebooks that they realise that the house owes its existence to a shipyard! Even so it seems implausible that this quiet valley, so far from the sea, could have once been a busy port.

Yet throughout the Middle Ages Smallhythe was the port for the town of Tenterden which stands two miles away. Tenterden was a member of the Cinque Ports Confederation and one of its claims to membership was that it had a port. The River Rother was a wide navigable channel throughout the medieval period, but when in 1287 a storm changed the course of its mouth from New Romney to Rye the whole of its valley started a slow process of change. One of the major signs was the gradual silting up of the channel to Smallhythe. However, as late as the

Smallhythe Place, originally the Harbour-Masters House.

71

reign of Henry VIII large ships were being built there, and goods loaded and unloaded at the little quay that may still be traced by the garden of Smallhythe Place. Even in Ellen Terry's day some goods were brought by boat, but now the watercourse is little more than a ditch.

Smallhythe Place was built in about 1515 as the Harbour-Master's House. It stood apart from the huddle of artisan's cottages and warehouses that made up the little port. Although there is some suggestion that the house is earlier it seems most unlikely as a serious fire in July 1514 destroyed the port, and it does not seem possible that a timber house such as this could have survived such a disasterous fire.

Just above the house is a charming little church built of brick at about the same time to replace a medieval one lost in the fire.

Places of Interest in the Neighbourhood
The Cause of the Goodwin Sands (Tenterden)
Two's Company (Biddenden)
The Pagan Altar in a Christian Church (Stone in Oxney)

The romantic ruins of St Mary's Church, Eastwell.

41 The Incognito King

Position: Eastwell lies to the NW of Ashford
Map reference: Sheet 189; 010473
Access: St Marys Church ruins stand by the Lake.

Few English Kings have aroused as much interest as Richard III. Most people believe that he was either very good, or very bad, but few would fail to agree that the days of the Plantagenets in the fifteenth century were numbered and that sooner or later the Tudors would have succeeded them to the throne.

As every schoolboy will tell you Richard III was killed at the Battle of Bosworth on 22nd August 1485, and our story at Eastwell starts just prior to the battle. A young boy called Richard, who had been brought up by a private tutor and unaware of the identity of his parents was ushered to an army encampment. There he met Richard III who told him that he was his natural father, and that should anything happen to him the boy must flee as any child of the king, illegitimate or not, would be sought out and murdered. As history records the king was killed and the young Richard fled to Kent where he settled at Eastwell.

Here he worked on the estate of Sir Thomas Moyle. After some years he gained Sir Thomas Moyle's confidence and told him of the events of 1485. Sir Thomas had already realised that there was something different about this boy as he had caught him reading books in his library – at a time when few could read and write. Sir Thomas believed his tale and granted him a small house on the estate and a pension. Here Richard lived in semi-secrecy for the rest of his life.

When he died in December 1550 he was buried in a place of honour on the north side of the altar at the church in Eastwell Park. The church register records his burial: Richard Plantagenet was buryed the 22nd daye of December anno ut supra ex registro de Eastwell sub anno 1550.

After the last war, when Eastwell Park had been under military control, and little maintenance had been carried out, the church at Eastwell collapsed. It is now a controlled ruin, lovingly cared for by a Charitable Trust, drawing thousands of tourists every year to see the burial place of the last of the Plantagenets.

Places of Interest in the Neighbourhood
Some Unique Volunteers (Ashford)
For Priests or Pests? (Great Chart)
An Eventful Life (Wye)

42 The Legend of Grey Dolphin

Position: The village of Eastchurch is on the Isle of Sheppey
Map reference: Sheet 178; 995715
Access: The ruins of Shurland Hall are not accessible, but may be seen
from a distance. The Shurland monument may be seen in Minster
Abbey Church.

One of the most famous legends in the county is that of Sir Robert de
Shurland and his horse, Grey Dolphin.

Just outside the village of Eastchurch stand the ruins of a large and
impressive house called Shurland. The present ruins are of a house built
in the early part of the sixteenth century for the Cheyne family, but the
site is far older, the Cheynes having inherited it from the Norman de
Shurland family.

Sir Robert de Shurland, crusader, Warden of the Cinque Ports and
advisor to King Edward I, lived at Eastchurch. He is buried in the
Abbey Church at Minster (he was also Lord of Minster and Baron
Sheppey), where his effigy may be seen in the south aisle. At his feet can
clearly be seen a carved horse's head – the same head that features in
the legend.

We are told that Sir Roger had been a hard landlord on Sheppey, and
that seeing the king's barge moored in the Swale estuary decided to ride
out to receive the king's pardon for all his wrong doings. On his return
he was accosted by an old witch who told him that 'that horse which has
saved your soul will one day be the death of you'. Not wishing to put it
to the test he killed the horse there and then. Some time later he was
walking on the beach with some friends when he saw his horse's skull
sticking out of the water. Not wishing to be reminded of the poor beast
he kicked it into the sea, but as he did so a piece of bone pierced his foot
and he died from blood poisoning!

How much of the legend is based on fact we cannot say. It was
first told in the seventeenth century, but in the nineteenth century
the romantic novelist Richard Barham reprinted it in his *Ingoldsby
Legends* giving the horse a name – Grey Dolphin.

All we can say with certainty is that there must have been a very good
reason for carving a horse's head on Sir Rogers tomb in 1310. It has
been pointed out that in the Middle Ages the symbol of a horse's head
denoted that you had the right to collect flotsam washed up around
your shore, and perhaps the legend is true so far as the trip out to the
king's barge is concerned. Was he going to ask the King's permission to

Sir Robert de Shurland's tomb, complete with horse's head!

collect driftwood? Maybe, but that would not explain why the Abbey Church chose to place a Horse's Head on its weathervane in the eighteenth century – a weathervane that has recently been discovered in the churchyard.

Places of Interest in the Neighbourhood
The Ship on the Shore (Minster on Sea)
Off like a Rocket! (Milton Regis)
Where Wellington Got his Powder (Faversham)

43 Tunnels of Dubious Origin

Position: Chislehurst Caves, near Chislehurst BR Station.
Map reference: Sheet 177; 432695
Access: The caves are regularly open to the public.

Kent has more man-made underground passages than any other county. This is due to the fact that the materials beneath our feet – chalk, sandstone, coal, are all of great practical and commercial use. It would be fair to say that for as long as man has been building in Kent he has also been digging into it.

One of the most interesting sites accessible to the public are the Chislehurst Caves, best known for having accommodated tens of thousands of Londoners during the last war.

There may be some older parts, but the vast majority of passages at Chislehurst date from the late eighteenth and nineteenth centuries as the use of chalk for mixing with sand to make mortar increased.

During the last War over 9000 people stayed nightly in Chislehurst Caves, travelling from London by special train. For the privilege of a safe night's sleep they paid 1d each, and were given an allotted bunk bed, the numbers of which may still be seen painted on the walls. In addition to the bed they had access to many amenities, including a cinema, chapel and hospital. However, if they were absent from their bunk for four nights or more it was re-allocated, and they were not allowed to let their bunks to anyone else. The camaraderie in the tunnels was exceptional, with many firm friendships being forged. Tales of the size of the tunnels abounded. A large map was painted on the entrance wall in order that residents shouldn't end up in the wrong bunk, and the generally accepted length of the passages was 22 miles, although in reality there were only about 10 miles in this part of the mine.

Places of Interest in the Neighbourhood
Where the Eagle Landed (Chislehurst)
The Lost View (Bexleyheath)
Where the Rake made Little Progress (Bexley)

44 Lord Darnley's White Elephant

Position: Cobham Mausoleum stands in Cobham Park
Map reference: Sheet 178; 695685
Access: The Mausoleum stands on a public footpath.

During the eighteenth century many fine mausolea were constructed by wealthy families to receive their mortal remains, and the remains of their descendants. In Kent there are three important buildings – at Chiddingstone, Farningham and Cobham.

The Cobham Mausoleum was built by the 4th Earl of Darnley in 1783. It was designed by the notable architect James Wyatt, to stand on a hill about a mile to the south of the house, and to be visible from it. Wyatt planned a square building with a pyramidal roof, entirely built of

The Darnley Mausoleum in Cobham Park.

brick and Portland stone. The accommodation provided for a chapel raised just above ground level, and a burial vault on the lower ground floor containing places for thirty two coffins.

For some reason – and there are still a variety of theories – the Mausoleum was never used. A mausoleum must be consecrated and, when the building was completed, Lord Darnley invited the Bishop of Rochester to perform the ceremony. The reply came back that the Bishop would be happy to perform the consecration – at a price! It is possible that Lord Darnley thought he had spent enough already, and decided there and then to abandon the project. There may have been a long running argument between the Darnleys and the Bishop that is no longer evident.

In any event, in 1790 Humphry Repton was commissioned to landscape the park, and he chose to make the Mausoleum one of the principal eyecatchers in the landscape, so it eventually served its purpose.

As it had never been used for burials, and was costly to maintain, it slowly fell into disrepair to the extent that by the 1980s it was in danger of falling down completely. In order to ensure its preservation planning permission was granted to turn it into a private residence, although this idea has yet to reach fruition.

Cobham Hall is an independent Girl's School and is open to the public at advertised times during the holidays.

Places of Interest in the Neighbourhood
The Murder at Dadd's Hole (Cobham)
The Lost Village (Dode)
Where did Dickens spend his Honeymoon? (Chalk)

45 A Little Bit of the East Comes West

Position: Chiddingstone lies to the West of Tonbridge
Map reference: Sheet 188; 497452
Access: Chiddingstone Castle is open to the public at advertised times during the summer.

The beautiful half timbered village of Chiddingstone is one of those 'typically English' villages that picture postcards portray so well. Often these villages have a Manor House, or Castle, and Chiddingstone has a good example of a nineteenth century Gothic revival castle, built around parts of an earlier Tudor house. The grounds were also remodelled in the picturesque style and some authentic-looking 'smugglers caves' constructed.

In 1955 the Castle was bought by Denys Eyre Bower to house his collections of works of art. Mr Bower had made a particular study of Eastern art and thought that Chiddingstone would make an ideal gallery. He did not want to create a museum, rather a private collection, in the style of eighteenth and nineteenth century travellers who went on the Grand Tour.

Today students of art visit the Castle from all over the world to see the galleries, which house the largest collection of Japanese lacquerwork displayed in the West. There are groups of medicine boxes, Netsuke ware, armour, Buddhist art and Egyptian rooms, including a mummified cat!

In addition to the Eastern Studies there is a vast collection of documents, pictures and artefacts associated with the Royal House of Stuart. It is claimed that this is the largest collection outside that housed at Windsor, and contains items of national importance including Lely's portrait of Nell Gwynne.

It may seem incongruous, but here, housed in a typical English mansion is one of the most exotic collections in the country.

Places of Interest in the Neighbourhood
An American's Tudor Village (Hever)
An Inventor Extraordinaire (Southborough)
Lord Sackville's Birdhouse (Sevenoaks)

46 The Created History House

Position: Kingsgate lies on the coast between Broadstairs and Margate
Map reference: Sheet 179; 397707
Access: All the follies are privately owned, but most may be seen from
the footpaths crossing the area.

Kingsgate is a remote part of Kent even today. In the eighteenth
century when it was purchased by Lord Holland it was even more so.
Lord Holland had been Paymaster General to the Forces and after
he bought it he built himself a magnificent house, part of which
still survives as a white painted building overlooking the bay. Once
complete, he furnished it with antique statues imported from Greece
and Italy. In order to gain an English dimension to the collection he
began to construct a series of picturesque buildings in the grounds,
including two cliff top castles. One, behind the Almshouse, was called
the Neptune Tower and was based on Henry VIIIs castles at Walmer
and Deal. On the opposite clifftop was a much larger castle which
formed Lord Holland's stables. It was built of flint and dressed stone
with towers and turrets. In the early part of this century it was enlarged
and has been converted for residential use.

Places of Interest in the Neighbourhood
The Empty Chair in an Airy Nest (Broadstairs)
The Eighth Wonder of the World (Margate)
The World's Largest Public Air Raid Shelter (Ramsgate)

The impressive elevation of Kingsgate Castle.

47 The Man who Attended his Own Funeral

Location: Scotney Castle, Lamberhurst
Map reference: Sheet 188; 689353
Access: Scotney Castle is owned by the National Trust and is open at advertised times during the summer.

There are few less likely places to find a medieval castle. Scotney lies in a deep valley on a small island created by damming the River Bewl. It was built in 1379 by Roger Ashburnham to protect the valley from incursions by the French who had sacked Rye and Hastings a few years earlier.

After the Reformation the Darells who lived in the Castle kept the 'Old Faith' and were one of the notable recusant families in southern England. A later Darell with a curious tale is Arthur, who died in 1720. At his funeral a man in a dark cloak muttered to one of the mourners 'that is me they are burying'. Nothing more was thought of this man, who walked away soon afterwards. But many years later the grave was reopened and it was found that Arthur Darell's coffin had burst open, and that it had been full of stones. To this day people cannot explain what happened to Arthur Darell, and whether the man at the funeral was Arthur, making sure that his plan wasn't discovered.

Places of Interest in the Neighbourhood
Margery the Martyr (Pembury)
Home of 'Disgusted' (Tunbridge Wells)
Where the Prisoners were not Well (Sissinghurst)

48 Where the Water Gushed Forth

Position: Otford Village is north of Sevenoaks
Map reference: Sheet 188; 528592
Access: Beckets Well is on Private Land. The Palace is on public land and can be visited.

The village of Otford had a busy medieval history. It lay on the so-called Pilgrims Way, one of many routes used by pilgrims on their way to the shrine of Becket in Canterbury Cathedral.

Otford had been part of the estates of the Archbishops of Canterbury since the eighth century, and a Manor House had always existed there.

It seems that in the twelfth century Thomas a Becket stayed here and was told that there was no adequate water supply. He walked out into a field near the Manor and struck the ground, whereupon water gushed forth. This is told in a story written by the first county historian, William Lambarde in the sixteenth century, when Becket's credibility was at an all time low following the Reformation. Lambarde goes on to tell us that Becket forbade nightingales to sing in Otford as one had disturbed his prayers, and that no smithy should prosper after one of his horses hooves was badly shod!

The Well survives in the grounds of a private house. It was excavated some years ago, and revealed to be a fourteenth century 'Holy Well' or place of superstitious resort.

By the early sixteenth century the manor house at Otford had become a regular Ecclesiastical Palace and Archbishop William Warham gave orders that it be rebuilt. The red brick building, which was completed by 1518, was one of the largest in Kent, and it was here that Henry VIII lodged on his way to the Field of the Cloth of Gold in 1520. Twenty years later he seized it from the church, but it was never again used for more than storage. Within a few years it was a ruin. Today part of one range remains, most of it converted into cottages, and it is hard for the visitor today to imagine the importance of Otford before the death of Henry VIII.

Places of Interest in the Neighbourhood
Queen Anne's Bath House (Lullingstone)
Lord Sackville's Birdhouse (Sevenoaks)
A Needlewoman of Note (Ightham)

The ruins of Otford's medieval Palace.

49 The World's Largest Public Air Raid Shelter

Position: Ramsgate Town Centre
Map reference: Sheet 179; 385650
Access: The underground passages may be traced by following the manhole covers that hide the ventilation shafts.

Few would guess that Ramsgate has the world's largest public air raid shelter, capable of holding over 35,000 people. The town was joined to the main railway network in 1863. The station stood on the seafront near the Harbour, and was reached by a mile and a quarter long brick-lined tunnel. In 1926 a new station was constructed outside the town and the original station pulled down. Its site was leased to an amusement company, who in 1936 re-opened part of the old railway tunnel to run miniature trains in, lit by second-hand Blackpool Illuminations! Instead of running the whole length of the old tunnel they built a spur off to Hereson Road where a little station was opened. In 1939 the Council decided to utilise these two tunnels, extending them to encircle the town, providing a tunnel with 23 entrances that could accommodate the whole population in times of emergency.

The first part of the scheme was in operation by June 1939 when it was opened by the Duke of Kent. The main tunnel ran from West Harbour via Queen Street, Cannon Road and Boundary Road where it joined the former Railway Tunnel at East Cliff. The average depth of tunnel was 67feet. At regular intervals small ventilator pipes ran up to the pavements, although some of these had to be blocked when it was realised that the draught below would be too strong to allow people to stand up!

One visitor was Winston Churchill. As he was about to enter the Mayor noticed that he was smoking one of his famous cigars and he politely explained that smoking was not allowed in the tunnels. Churchill took it from his mouth and threw it onto the sanded floor. 'There goes a good'un,' are the words he is reported to have uttered!

After the war the tunnels were gradually sealed off, but the entrances in both East and West Cliffs may be seen, and the entrances in the town, now covered with concrete rafts, are unmistakable.

Places of Interest in the Neighbourhood
The Created History House (Kingsgate)
The Kentish Sampson (St Peters in Thanet)
The Empty Chair in an Airy Nest (Broadstairs)

84

50 Women, Officers and Soldiers

Position: The Grand Shaft, Dover
Map reference: Sheet 179; 315403
Access: The Grand Shaft is administered by Dover Museum and is
open to the public at advertised times during the summer.

The Western Heights at Dover were one of the largest areas of army
occupation at the start of the nineteenth century. France was then at
war with England, and Napoleon threatened to invade. The Castle, on
the Eastern Heights, was already crammed full of troops, so it was
decided to build an even larger fortification on the Western Heights.
Huge areas of the hillside were dug out to provide underground
fortresses larger than anything that had been built in England before. In
1823 the writer William Cobbett noted that over 2 square miles of
clifftops had been honeycombed, and that enough bricks had been used
in the fortifications to house every man woman and child in Kent.

The major disadvantage to being situated on the clifftop was a feeling
of being 'cut off' from the town and harbour. To this end a remarkable
structure known as the Grand Shaft' was constructed to link the clifftop
with the sea.

The shaft was designed by Sir Thomas Hyde Page and built in 1802. It
consists of three staircases built around an open shaft. Each staircase
revolves around the outside wall of the shaft, which provides light and
air, but each staircase remains a separate structure. It meant that large
numbers of men could be moved up and down very quickly.

During peacetime it was available for the entire garrison and their
families to use, and it is reputed that there was one staircase each for
Women, Officers and Others! In 1812 someone rode a horse up one of
the staircases to prove a bet. The stairs are not steep, but there are a lot
of them!

Places of Interest in the Neighbourhood
Where the Romans got their Directions (Dover)
The Finest Eighteenth Century Ensemble (Waldershare)
Memorial to a Physician of Note (Folkestone)

51 The Sorry Tale of Thomas Arden

Position: Arden's House, Abbey Street, Faversham
Map reference: Sheet 178; 018618
Access: Arden's House is privately owned and not open to the public.

Arden's House is one of the few reminders of the magnificent Faversham Abbey built in 1147 by King Stephen, at 400 feet long one of the largest Norman monastic buildings ever constructed. After the Reformation the church was destroyed, its stone being used as convenient rubble for towns folk to use. However, the Outer Gatehouse, built in the thirteenth century, survived complete demolition and now forms part of Arden's House.

Thomas Arden purchased the remains of Faversham Abbey soon after its closure. He was a prominent citizen of the town, serving as its Mayor in 1547, and he converted the former gateway of the Abbey into a comfortable residence for his wife Alice and himself.

Unknown to Arden, Alice was having an affair with a man called Mosbie. The two plotted to get rid of Arden by fair means or foul, and engaged some ruffians, Black Will and Shakebag, to murder him. On the 15th February 1551 he was murdered in his own house, just before he was due to host a dinner party, and his body stored in a cupboard whilst his wife entertained their guests, saying that her husband had been inexplicably delayed in London. His wife and her accomplices were subsequently arrested and executed.

Places of Interest in the Neighbourhood
Where Wellington got his Powder (Faversham)
Southern England's First Passenger Railway (Whitstable)
Off like a rocket! (Milton Regis)

52 Where Wellington got his Powder

Position: Chart Gunpowder Mills, Westbrook Walk, Faversham
Map reference: Sheet 178; 012617
Access: The Mills are maintained by the Faversham Society and are open to the public at advertised times during the summer.

It is obvious to see why Faversham was a suitable location for a Gunpowder Works. It was ideally placed as a port, it had access to the extensive woodlands of the Weald of Kent for charcoal, and had a good water supply. Saltpetre and sulphur were imported by boat, and the finished gunpowder exported by boats for reasons of safety. Quite when the gunpowder industry moved to Faversham is unclear, but it was probably during the latter part of the fifteenth century.

The making of gunpowder was a dangerous business. Explosions were always possible, and attempts were made to lessen the effects should an accident occur. Trees were planted around the works to soften any explosion, and heavy leather 'curtains' used inside the buildings to counter any blasts.

Indeed there were several serious explosions, one of which occurred in April 1781 when 3 tons of gunpowder went up, damaging many buildings in the town. It was lucky that only 3 people were killed, but

Chart Gunpowder Mills, just outside Faversham town centre.

nevertheless the explosion was heard as far away as London. It is said that one of the reasons Faversham's church tower was rebuilt in the eighteenth century with an openwork spire was to lessen the resistance in case there was an explosion.

The gunpowder produced at the Royal Works in Faversham would have been used by Nelson at Trafalgar and Wellington at Waterloo.

The mills closed in 1934 and most of the site was demolished, but in 1969 the Faversham Society started a project of restoration with the intention of opening the surviving buildings to the public.

Places of Interest in the Neighbourhood
The Sorry Tale of Thomas Arden (Faversham)
Off like a rocket! (Milton Regis)
Southern England's First Passenger Railway (Whitstable)

The first breakthrough of the Channel Tunnel in 1990.

53 A Tunnel under the Channel

Position: The Channel Tunnel, Shakespeare Cliff, Dover
Map reference: Sheet 179; 295390
Access: The Eurotunnel Exhibition Centre at St Martins Plain,
Cheriton, is open regularly throughout the year.

Attempts to dig a tunnel under the Channel date back to 1802 when a
French mining engineer came up with the idea of a fixed link between
England and the Continent. It was to be a single tunnel running under
the sea bed, and coming up on an island that would have been constructed in mid-Channel. Horses would have pulled carriages through
the oil-lit tunnel, which would have been ventilated by chimneys poking
up above water level! Not surprisingly the plans got little further than
the drawing board.

Thirty years later more plans were drawn up by the French, and a
full geological survey carried out, which seemed to show that a bridge
would be a more practical alternative. Money was not forthcoming and
the project was put on ice.

Sir Edward Watkin MP, chairman of three railway companies, was
the prime mover in the Channel Tunnel Company, and in 1880 digging
commenced in both England and France, but once again the scheme
folded through lack of funds.

The present works may be clearly seen from a public footpath on
Shakespeare Cliff at Dover, whilst at Cheriton a permanent display
shows the history of the tunnel from its conception to the present day.

Places of Interest in the Neighbourhood
A Physician of Note (Folkestone)
Where a Dastardly Plot was Hatched (Saltwood)
The Disinterred Residents of Hythe (Hythe)

54 Where the Romans got their Directions

Position: The Pharos, Dover Castle
Map reference: Sheet 179; 325419
Access: The Pharos may be visited during normal Castle opening hours.

Standing within the Iron Age Hill fort that was the precursor of the present Dover Castle stands the tallest Roman structure in this country, the Pharos.

Guidebooks often refer to this remarkable tower as a lighthouse, but in reality it is a beacon turret – quite a different thing. Lighthouses warn ships off dangerous rocks, whilst the two Pharos at Dover were for guiding ships into harbour. The other Pharos stood on the Western Heights, but was demolished in the early nineteenth century when the Napoleonic fortifications were being built.

During the night a beacon would be kept blazing on the top of both towers and ships setting sail from the other side of the Channel would steer a course mid way between them to bring them directly into the safety of the Dour estuary. During the day smoke fires were lit to similarly act as a navigational aid.

Places of Interest in the Neighbourhood
Women, Officers and Soldiers (Dover)
The Finest Eighteenth Century Ensemble (Waldershare)
Where the Ball drops on Time (Deal)

The Roman Pharos in the grounds of Dover Castle.

55 The Church with Two Enemies

Position: Reculver Towers stand to the East of Herne Bay
Map reference: Sheet 179; 228695
Access: The Church is owned by English Heritage and is open at
advertised times during the summer.

This part of the coastline was first inhabited by the Romans in the third
century. They built a fort here, the remains of which may still be seen.
After their departure the fort fell into decay, and most of it has now
been eaten away by the sea. During the seventh century the area was
colonised by Christians who had been given the land by Egbert, King of
Kent. It was an ideal site as far as the monks were concerned as they
could raid the broken down Roman walls for stone with which to build
their small, seventy feet long church, which had a screen of two columns
separating nave from chancel. Throughout the Middle Ages it served as
a parish church for the area.

It must always have been an inhospitable piece of coastline, with the
churchyard constantly threatened by the sea, which erodes here at a
rapid rate. Yet the church had another enemy, an early nineteenth century vicar. His mother apparently took a dislike to the church – or more
probably to the journey to it – and persuaded him to pull it down.

Luckily Trinity House stepped in before demolition of the old church
was complete. They purchased the west towers and preserved them as
aids to navigation.

Places of Interest in the Neighbourhood
Southern England's First Passenger Railway (Whitstable)
The Forgotten Port (Fordwich)
A Campanologist's Dream (Birchington)

56 Home of 'Disgusted'

Position: The Pantiles, Royal Tunbridge Wells
Map reference: Sheet 188; 581387
Access: During the summer the waters may be tasted in the Pantiles.

In 1606 Dudley, Lord North, was travelling from Eridge when he chanced upon a spring. He took a sip – and the town of Tunbridge Wells was born. After all, any water that could taste that bad must be good for you!

The local landowner, Lord Bergavenny, paved the spring and it became a popular place for day visitors who stayed at Tonbridge, the nearest town. In the summer of 1630 Henrietta Maria, Queen of Charles I stayed at these wells in preference to those at Bath, and had to camp out on the common as there were no lodging houses close by. After that visitors were much more frequent and houses were built to serve them. Certainly by the 1630s they were known as 'Tonbridge Wells' (the spelling was changed much later when the town had become established as an entity on its own).

A frequent visitor at the end of the century was Princess (later Queen) Anne. In 1698 her son slipped off the gravel walk that lead to the Wells, and the generous Princess gave £100 for the area to be paved. The following year she returned and was disgusted to find that nothing had been done. Was she the original 'Disgusted of Tunbridge Wells', we wonder?

Places of Interest in the Neighbourhood
An Inventor Extraordinaire (Southborough)
Margery the Martyr (Pembury)
The Man who Attended his Own Funeral (Lamberhurst)

A glimpse of The Pantiles, looking towards the Spring.

57 The Finest Eighteenth Century Ensemble in Kent

Position: Waldershare Park lies to the north of Dover
Map reference: Sheet 179; 281476
Access: The Park is crossed by Public Footpaths. The House is privately occupied and not accessible. The Belvedere is under restoration and is not open, but the Church may be visited by arrangement with the Estate Office.

Waldershare Park is the seat of the Earl of Guilford. It is a marvellously quiet place within striking distance of the bustling port of Dover. At its heart is the Mansion House built in the first decade of the eighteenth century for Sir Henry Furnese.

Standing in the Park, and almost certainly never completed, stands the greatest of the eighteenth century estate buildings, the Belvedere, built in 1725 for Sir Robert Furnesse. It seems to have been designed by Lord Burlington as a Music Room. No doubt its marvellous first floor room was also intended as a Banqueting Hall in the manner of, say, the Worcester Lodge at Badminton. The plum coloured bricks used in its construction were made locally, but even so the then cost of £1700 seems reasonable for such a gigantic building. After suffering two hundred years of neglect it is being restored.

No other country estate in Kent offers such a grouping of eighteenth century work, and Waldershare deserves to be better known.

Places of Interest in the Neighbourhood
Where the Ball drops on Time (Deal)
Women, Officers and Soldiers (Dover)
Where the Romans got their Directions (Dover)

58 The Cause of the Goodwin Sands

Position: St Mildreds Church, Tenterden
Map reference: Sheet 189; 884333
Access: The church is in the town centre

The parish church at Tenterden is dedicated to St Mildred (see Minster) and may denote that there was a church here in the eighth century. However, the present church is basically fourteenth and fifteenth century, the medieval building being completed by the erection of the present tower between 1450 and 1500.

  Legend tells us that this tower was the 'cause' of the Goodwin Sands, the notorious sandbanks in the English Channel. In the mid sixteenth century a commission was established to find out why Sandwich Haven had silted up – a process that was thought to be linked with the growth of the Goodwin Sands. Members of the Commission were sent out to all the Cinque Ports and their associate towns, including Tenterden, and here an old man was found sitting on the churchyard wall. Upon asking him why Sandwich Haven had silted up he told the enquirer that when he was a boy, prior to the building of the tower behind him, the Goodwin Sands had posed few problems. This story reached London and poor Tenterden tower has received the blame ever since!

Places of Interest in the Neighbourhood
Where Ships once Sailed across the Fields (Smallhythe)
The Largest Ditch in England (Appledore)
The Pagan Altar in a Christian Church (Stone in Oxney)

Tenterden Church Tower dates from the sixteenth century.

59 Poor William of Perth

Location: Rochester City Centre
Map reference: Sheet 178; 744686
Access: Black Boy Alley leads off the High Street opposite Lloyds
Bank. Rochester cathedral is open daily.

The narrow and draughty lane known as Black Boy Alley which leads
off Rochester High Street is a typical Pilgrim's Passage, so often found
in medieval cities. It was well used before the Reformation by pilgrims

The view down Black Boy Alley, Rochester.

visiting Rochester Cathedral, and its story starts in 1201 with the death of William of Perth.

To put the story into its historical context, Becket had been murdered at Canterbury thirty years earlier, and in the intervening years his shrine had become the most important place of pilgrimage in England. Pilgrims brought wealth and large sums could be accumulated if a church had a shrine. The monks at Rochester inevitably wished that they too could provide a shrine.

We know that in 1201 a baker called William, who had travelled down from Perth on his way to Canterbury, was murdered in Rochester, but the next part of the story is conjectural. Whether he was murdered by the monks, or by a robber is not known, but he was buried in the Cathedral church. Within a few months miracles started to occur at his tomb, and the Cathedral had its shrine. In 1256 William of Perth was canonised and Rochester was well on the way to filling its coffers.

By the middle of the century much of the Cathedral had been rebuilt using money left at William's shrine – and the rest would have been rebuilt as well had not a dispute between the townsfolk and the monks arisen over use of the building. This dispute was not finally settled until 1423 when the townsfolk built their own church to the north of the Cathedral.

So popular was the shrine of St William that a one-way system was devised for pilgrims. They would be ushered off Watling Street (the main London-Canterbury Road that is now the High Street) and down the little lane that is now called Black Boy Alley. Here they would enter the Cathedral at the north transept and proceed to William's shrine on their knees. The hollows made by their knees may still be seen in the stone staircase today. Having visited the shrine they would leave the cathedral at the South transept and go on their way rejoicing!

The shrine of St William is still to be seen in the north transept of Rochester Cathedral, next to the tomb of a more famous later benefactor, Walter de Merton, founder of Merton College, Oxford.

Places of Interest in the Neighbourhood
The City Centre Alpine Retreat (Rochester)
The Wet Railway (Strood)
A Tale of Two Stones (River Medway)

60 The Kentish Sampson

Position: St Peter's Church, Thanet
Map reference: Sheet 179; 370653
Access: The tomb is in the churchyard, near the main path.

At St Peter's Church near Broadstairs is the grave of Richard Joy, who was known during his lifetime as the 'Kentish Sampson.'
The inscription reads as follows:

> In Memory of Richard Joy
> called the Kentish Sampson
> Who died May 18th 1742 aged 67
> Herculean Hero, famed for strength,
> At last lies here, his breadth and length.
> See how the mighty man is fall'n,
> To death the strong and weak are all one,
> And the same judgement doth befall
> Goliath great, as David Small.

The story is told that Richard worked as a brewer's delivery man, and that one day whilst in London he went into a pub where he saw a leg of mutton roasting over the open fire. He asked the landlord to serve some to his fellow deliverymen, but just as the landlord was about to carve the meat off the spit some three or four gentlemen walked in the door and requested some mutton. The landlord told Richard that he and his friends would have to wait as the gentlemen would be served first. In response to which Richard picked the mutton off the fire and wrapped it, spit and all, around the unlucky landlord's neck! It was only then, we are told, that the landlord realised he had been talking to the Kentish Sampson!

Richard certainly came from a strong family. His father, Richard, had displayed his strength at the Duke of York Theatre in London in 1672 by lifting a weight of 2,240lbs, and his uncle William was equally as talented. In fact they both earned second incomes from performing feats of strength at fairs and markets.

One fact not recorded on Richard's tombstone is his death by drowning!

Places of Interest in the Neighbourhood
A Royal Playground (Margate)
The Created History House (Kingsgate)
The Empty Chair in an Airy Nest (Broadstairs)

61 A Trip to the Underworld

Position: Leeds Castle near Maidstone
Map reference: Sheet 188; 838533
Access: Leeds Castle is open to the public at advertised times
throughout the year.

Leeds Castle has been described as 'the most beautiful Castle in the
world', and since being opened to the public has become one of
England's top tourist attractions.

A visit to the new Grotto unfolds like a storybook. One enters the
Maze – its hedges still rather underdeveloped – and only when one has
reached the centre is it realised that there is a grotto underneath. As you
enter you hear the sound of rushing water, and pass the statues of the
Guardians of the Grot – an essential part of every good grotto. Once
inside the main chamber there are swans all over the ceiling, the huge
tufa face of Typhoeus dripping with water and near life size figures of
the Elements made out of coral and crystals, as well as a staircase of
bones which leads to a topsy-turvy world with fish on the roof and
upside down animals. A huge mother of pearl fish stands near a brick
waterfall.

The Grotto was built in the eighteenth century fashion in 1988 with all
sorts of materials, including slag, flint and Blue John.

Places of Interest in the Neighbourhood
The Volunteer's Memorial (Maidstone)
The Fire on the Heath (Penenden Heath)

Inside the newly constructed Grotto at Leeds Castle.

62 The Queer Quintain

Position: Offham Village
Map reference: Sheet 188; 656573
Access: The Quintain stands on the village green.

The Offham Quintain is the only one of its type to survive in England, yet every village must have had one in the Middle Ages.

The Quintain is a white painted post, approximately nine feet high with a cross piece attached to the top. This top piece is pivoted, so that it can revolve.

Offham's Quintain stands on the village green.

One end of the cross piece is wide and flat, like a paddle, whilst the other end is pointed, and has a wooden sausage shaped piece of wood suspended from it by a chain. The object of the Quintain was to practice horsemanship. No doubt it had its origins at a time when tournaments were popular, and gave plenty of opportunity for target practice using a lance. As tournaments went out of fashion the use of the Quintain was restricted to demonstrations, or local skill games.

The idea was to ride at the Quintain, to hit the paddle board and to get out of the way quickly, before the sausage shaped piece of wood swung round and hit you hard on the back of the head! It sounds dangerous, but in all probability the wooden sausage would have been substituted by a bag of sand most of the time, giving a hefty wallop without the risk of permanent damage!

Places of Interest in the Neighbourhood
Where a Deserter was Recaptured (Wrotham)
Where a Saint was Startled (West Malling)
Was Lady de Leybourne Heartless? (Leybourne)

Poor St Leonard – startled by Battle of Britain planes!

63 Where a Saint was Startled

Position: The hamlet of St Leonards, West Malling
Map reference: Sheet 188; 673566
Access: The Startled Saint stands on the Mereworth road. St Leonards
Tower is owned by English Heritage.

In about AD 1090 Bishop Gundulf of Rochester founded an Abbey in
the town of West Malling. It stands in Swan Street and is today the
home of Anglican nuns. Whilst it is not open to the public one may
catch a glimpse of the massive Norman Tower behind the gatehouse –
one of the few survivals of the original church. Gundulf also granted
lands to the nuns – some to be farmed by the community, other parts to
be let to produce an income.

To protect their scattered lands which stood at the other end of the
town Bishop Gundulf built a tower that would have maintained a small
band of men employed to stop pillagers seizing Abbey crops. The tower
dates from about 1100, and was built of local ragstone and tufa, on a
natural rocky ledge half a mile from the Abbey. It still stands, almost to
its full height, a strong and sturdy tower capable of showing potential
thieves that the Abbey lands were not to be tampered with.

The Abbey established a small chapel nearby, dedicated to St
Leonard. Today there is no trace of the chapel, but the saint's memory
is preserved elsewhere in the area. Just up the road from the tower is a
Public House called 'The Startled Saint'. It's comical sign shows poor St
Leonard raising his hands and eyes in horror as planes circle overhead –
a reminder that West Malling was an RAF Station and Battle of Britain
airfield.

Places of Interest in the Neighbourhood
The Queer Quintain (Offham)
Was Lady de Leybourne Heartless? (Leybourne)
A Little Bit of Old Italy (Mereworth)

64 Lord Sackville's Birdhouse

Position: Knole Park, Sevenoaks
Map reference: Sheet 188; 545539
Access: Knole Park is open daily throughout the year. The Mansion House is open at advertised times during the summer.

Knole House, which dates in the main from the early seventeenth century, is the seat of Lord Sackville, who can trace his descent from Thomas Sackville who held many Offices of State under Queen Elizabeth I. In the intervening years the family have held other titles, including the Earldom and Dukedom of Dorset. As the family grew in wealth and rank so the house and its environs were improved and extended to form the ensemble we see today.

Part of Knole Park is now a golf course, and on the edge of the course stands a charming little white painted building. It was originally erected in 1761 by Lionel, 1st Duke of Dorset, as a summer house. Architecturally, it is rustic Gothick and possibly incorporates some stonework from the demolished Otford Palace.

In the nineteenth century, it was turned into an Aviary, probably by Lord Amherst, brother in law of the 4th Duke of Dorset. Lord Amherst was a collector of exotic birds which he discovered during his several stints as English Ambassador in the Middle and Far East. One species of pheasant, *Phasianus amherstiae* was named after him. Today the little building is still known as the Aviary although it has been a long time since birds were kept there.

Places of Interest in the Neighbourhood
A Needlewoman of Note (Ightham)
Where the Water Gushed Forth (Otford)
Mr May's Folly (Hadlow)

The Bird House in Knole Park, Sevenoaks.

65 Where Shells Reign Supreme

Position: St James Church, Cooling
Map reference: Sheet 178; 756759
Access: The church is open daily.

Cooling Church has two claims to fame. Firstly, it was used as the setting for the opening scene of Dicken's novel *Great Expectations:* 'At such a time I found out that this bleak place overgrown with nettles was the churchyard, and that Philip Pirrip, late of this parish, and also Georgina, wife of the above, were dead and buried; and that Alexander, Bartholomew, Abraham and Tobias, and Roger, infant children of the aforesaid, were also dead and buried; and that the dark, flat wilderness beyond the churchyard, intersected with dykes, and mounds, and gates, with scattered cattle feeding on it, was the marshes; and that the low leaden line beyond was the river.'

The gravestones so evocatively described as belonging to Pip's family actually belong to the Comports, who lived in the area in the eighteenth century. The church gets a large number of visitors, especially from abroad, who want to savour the atmosphere they have tasted when reading the book.

The other reason that the church should be remembered is for its vestry. No other church in England can have one like this! It is tiny – just five feet by seven feet, but the walls are entirely covered with cockle shells to give the impression of a grotto. All the shells are local, probably collected in the Thames estuary. But who put them there and why remains a mystery. There are some initials and part of a date picked out near the top of the design, but it is sadly incomplete and offers little consolation to the enquirer.

Places of Interest in the Neighbourhood
A Red Indian Princess (Gravesend)
The Wet Railway (Strood)
Where did Dickens spend his Honeymoon? (Chalk)

66 For Priests or Pests?

Position: Great Chart, near Ashford
Map reference: Sheet 189; 979419
Access: The Pest House stands in front of the Parish Church.

By the churchyard gate stands a tiny timber framed house, probably built in the fifteenth or sixteenth century. It is known locally as 'The Pest House'. Such buildings were sometimes erected in the Middle Ages to accommodate villagers suffering from contagious diseases, including the plague.

It is however just as likely that it was originally built as a priest's house. In the medieval period many churches were endowed with Chantry Chapels – small chapels within the church that were adminis-

The tiny Pest House outside Great Chart Church.

tered separately to the rest of the building. The parish priest, who was usually resident in the village, would have no control over the priest who was licensed to say Mass in the Chantry Chapel. The chantry priest was only responsible to the trustees of the benefactor's estate. Chantry priests would be paid per Mass, usually one a week in each chantry, for a set number of years, and clever priests collected Chantries – serving one or two a day in different parts of the area, and amassing quite an income in the process. Because they were permanently on the move, lodgings like the Pest House at Great Chart were their only accommodation. We know from the records that a chantry did exist at Great Chart, established by James Goldwell, Bishop of Norwich in 1475, the right date for the little house next door.

Places of Interest in the Neighbourhood
Some Unique Volunteers (Ashford)
The Incognito King (Eastwell)
An Eventful Life (Wye)

The plaque recording the events of June 1799 in Wrotham village.

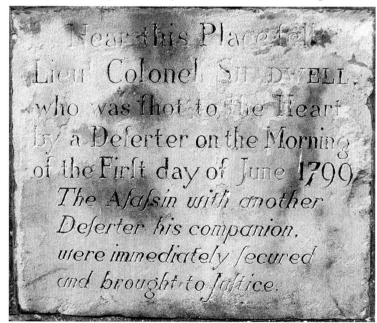

67 Where a Deserter was Recaptured

Position: Wrotham village lies to the West of Maidstone
Map reference: Sheet 188; 613592
Access: The Plaque can be seen next to the Bull Inn.

During the late eighteenth and early nineteenth centuries Kent became a large army training and mustering area.The prime area chosen for the encampments was Cocks Heath (today Coxheath) on the sandstone ridge that runs to the south of Maidstone.It was a large, dry, and relatively flat area of heathland, ideal for tented soldiers. The earliest recorded camp there was of Hanoverian soldiers in 1756, but they were a troublesome lot and didn't get on very well with the residents of Maidstone. Later in the century the war in the American colonies caused the Reserve Militia to be called out and fifteen thousand troops were stationed here.

The threat of a Napoleonic invasion at the end of the eighteenth century meant that if France was going to invade it would be via Romney Marsh, so it was important to have large numbers of men stationed close enough to the coast to deal quickly with all eventualities. Once again Cocks Heath was called into service, and a so called 'Volunteer' Brigade was formed. It is certain that not all those who joined did so out of choice. Many were forced into it by their employers who needed to be seen to support the patriotic movement, but who didn't want to have to send money. So they sent their poorly paid and 'dispensable' servants. Many of these servants greatly resented this treatment and absconded from the Brigade. Two such deserters made a run for it from Cocks Heath and made it as far as the village of Wrotham at the foot of the North Downs in June 1799. Here they were apprehended, but not before one of them had fatally shot Lt Col Shadwell, one of the officers sent to detail them.

A plaque recording the event is still to be seen near the spot where the officer fell, outside the Bull Inn. The inscription ends with these words: 'The assassin with another deserter, his companion, were immediately secured and brought to justice'.

Places of Interest in the Neighbourhood
The Lost Village (Dode)
The Queer Quintain (Offham)
A Needlewoman of Note (Ightham)

68 The Volunteer's Memorial

Position: Mote Park stands to the East of Maidstone Town Centre
Map reference: Sheet 188; 775544
Access: Mote Park is a Public Open Space, open daily.

It has often been said that Maidstone's greatest asset is Mote Park, a 450 acre public open space that surrounds Mote House, former seat of the Earl of Romney.

On one of the slopes overlooking the lake stands a small Greek temple, erected in 1801 as a memorial to Lord Romney from the Kentish Volunteers. It carries an inscriptions as follows:

> This Pavilion was erected by the Volunteers of Kent as a tribute
> of respect to the Earl of Romney, Lord Lieutenant of the County,
> MDCCCI

On August 1st 1799 the 5,000 men of the Volunteer Brigades assembled on these slopes to show their loyalty to Lord Romney. In addition to the troops 20,000 spectators had turned out to catch a glimpse of George III and Queen Charlotte. As they entered the Park guns were fired and the review of troops commenced. Then the royal party retired to a marquee to receive an address from the Corporation, after which Lord Romney served a veritable feast consisting of 60 lambs, 700 fowls, 300 hams, 220 dishes of beef, 220 meat pies, 220 joints of veal, 220 fruit pies. No wonder it was decided to thank Lord Romney for his benevolence! The next day there was enough food left over to hand out to 600 starving Maidstonians!

Places of Interest in the Neighbourhood
The Fire on the Heath (Penenden Heath)
A Trip to the Underworld (Leeds)

The Pavilion erected in Mote Park by the Kentish Volunteers.

69 A Red Indian Princess and her Happy Hunting Ground

Position: St George's Church, Gravesend
Map reference: Sheet 177; 646743
Access: The statue stands in St George's Churchyard.

Gravesend must once have been a lovely place. It's name is derived from Groves End – where the woods reached the River Thames.

Unfortunately there is little early history left. The town was devastated by a fire in 1727 and nearly all the buildings in the town centre date from the rebuilding, including the parish church of St George, paid for by Parliament.

The former St Georges Church, on the same site as the present building, was the burial place of Princess Pocahontas, an American Indian who died in 1617. Pocahontas was living in Virginia when an English expedition lead by Captain John Smith arrived. She fell in love with him, saving him from a scalping at the hands of her tribe. Whilst he was grateful to her for saving his life he hurriedly left for Jamestown. Unknown to him she followed his trail, and although he had set sail by the time she reached Jamestown, she waited for his certain return. Whilst waiting for Smith she met another Englishman, John Rolfe, whom she married and bore a son. In 1616 Rolfe set sail for England, bringing his new family with him. Whilst in London Pocahontas was presented at Court where she met James I.

England wasn't at all as Pocahontas had imagined, and she longed to return to Virginia. In the spring of 1617 she persuaded her husband to let her go back, and laden with gifts from members of the Court she set sail from London for the long passage home. It was whilst waiting for the ship to leave the Thames at Gravesend that she succumbed to an English cold, from which she died.

Pocahontas was buried in St George's Church in Gravesend, although after the fire of 1727 the exact place of her burial was lost.

Places of Interest in the Neighbourhood
Where did Dickens spend his Honeymoon? (Chalk)
The Murder at Dadd's Hole (Cobham)
Where Shells Reign Supreme (Cooling)

(For illustration see Frontispiece)

70 A Tale of Two Stones

Position: The River Medway
Map reference: Sheet 178; 720669
Access: The London Stone is on the riverbank at Lower Upnor.

No-one would imagine that the muddy waters of the River Medway at
Rochester could possibly have been the cause of major battles. Yet this
portion of the Medway was always under dispute for its profitable fishing rights.

The City of Rochester held the rights over the portion near the City.
They stretched as far upstream as the Hawkwood Stone, which may still
be seen between Rochester and Aylesford. This was the boundary
between the fishermen of Rochester and Maidstone, and seems to
have remained relatively undisputed over the centuries. Rochester's
problems came with the fishing rights at the other extremity, and
revolved around a boundary known as the London Stone, which stands
near Upnor.

As its name suggests the altercations were between the fishermen of
Rochester and those of the Corporation of London. Rochester claimed
rights over the Medway as far downstream as Sheerness, whilst the
Londoners claimed rights over the Medway as far upstream as Upnor,
leaving a large area of disputed river in the middle!

Places of Interest in the Neighbourhood
The City Centre Alpine Retreat (Rochester)
The Lost Village (Dode)
A Machine for the Drowned (Aylesford)

London Stone at Upnor.

71 The Lost View

Position: Danson Park, Bexleyheath
Map reference: Sheet 177; 475753
Access: Danson Park is a public open space and open daily. Chapel Cottage is a private residence and not open.

The Mansion House at Danson Park was built to the designs of Sir Robert Taylor in 1760 for John Boyd. It was to serve as Boyd's country house, his main residence being in London, but today one would hardly imagine that Danson had ever been in the country!

With the new mansion completed, Boyd ordered the demolition of the old house that he had bought with the estate, after which he called in Lancelot Brown to landscape the park. Brown suggested damming the small river to form a lake on the site of the old house – thus covering the foundations that would otherwise have scarred the view.

A bridge and garden temple were constructed, and the nearby road realigned to give a sense of space. The temple no longer stands at Danson, having been sold earlier this century and re-erected in the lovely gardens of the Bury at St Pauls Walden in Hertfordshire. With the landscaping planned Boyd handed the designs to his gardener, Fean Garwood, who carried out the instructions. Garwood is buried at St Marys Churchyard in nearby Bexley, and the trees in Danson Park remain as a memorial to him. As an outward sign that he was a man of culture, Boyd purchased a huge antique urn, made for the Emperor Hadrian, but this too no longer survives at Danson, having been re-erected in the Orangery at Kensington Palace.

To further improve the view from the Park, Boyd adapted a little cottage near Blendon by giving it a Spire. From the house it looked like a little chapel on the hill. That 'Chapel Cottage' still stands near the junction of the A210 and B2210, but it can no longer be seen from the Mansion House as twentieth century suburbia and the A2 dual carriageway have now filled in the parkland between the two buildings.

Places of Interest in the Neighbourhood
Where the Rake made Little Progress (Bexley)
Where the Eagle Landed (Chislehurst)
Tunnels of Dubious Origin (Chislehurst)

Chapel Cottage, Blendon.

72 The Hartlake Bridge Disaster

Position: Hartlake Bridge and Hadlow Churchyard, both near Tonbridge
Map reference: Sheet 188; 629472 (bridge) 635498 (memorial)
Access: Hartlake Bridge lies on the minor road from Golden Green to Tudeley.

The portion of the Medway valley between Tonbridge and Maidstone has always formed the centre of the English hop industry.

In the autumn of 1853 some hop pickers were working in gardens near Golden Green, on the outskirts of Hadlow. Following heavy rain the River Medway burst its banks near Hartlake Bridge, which lay on their route back to their huts at Tudeley. The farmer for whom they were working sent two waggons to collect them, but they reached Hartlake Bridge to find the river had risen so much that only the wooden rails along the parapet were still visible. One waggon safely crossed the flooded river, but when the second was on the bridge one of its horses slipped, and the waggon hit the parapet rail which gave way, throwing its occupants into the river. With the force of flood water all the victims were quickly washed away and of the forty or so people on the waggon, thirty died, many of their bodies not being recovered for several weeks.

The victims were buried in the south-eastern corner of Hadlow Churchyard, their funerals being paid for by the Medway Navigation Company, who also paid for Hartlake Bridge to be rebuilt in stone.

Places of Interest in the Neighbourhood
Margery the Martyr (Pembury)
Home of 'Disgusted' (Tunbridge Wells)
An Inventor Extraordinaire (Southborough)

Hartlake Bridge replaced that destroyed by floods in 1853.

73 A Room with a View

Position: Romney Marsh
Map reference: Sheet 189; 060300
Access: There are several Lookers Huts on the Marsh, although
most are now in ruins.

Romney Marsh is the generic name for a group of Marshes that have
been reclaimed from the Sea. Much of the reclamation was carried out
under Monastic influence during the Middle Ages with the sole purpose
of providing excellent grazing lands.

Over the centuries a particular breed of sheep was created that could
put up with the special conditions of the area, which could be bleak and
frequently under water. This breed, the *Kent*, or *Romney Marsh*, is one
of the most popular throughout the world.

Whilst the breed could be developed to cope with the conditions, the
shepherds who tended them needed a certain amount of comfort. Often
they would have to stay out overnight, as even short distances across
the Marsh take a long time. To facilitate the overnight stays the
shepherds built small brick huts in the more isolated areas, containing
bunk beds and a tiny fireplace. Many of these survive, and although
most date from the nineteenth century they are nearly all ruined. The
local name for a shepherd was 'looker' and these 'Looker's Huts' still
pepper the landscape of dykes and marshes.

Places of Interest in the Neighbourhood
The Shocked Steeple (Brookland)
Where the Wheels Run Smoothly (New Romney)
The Largest Ditch in England (Appledore)

74 Dane John's Dungeon

Position: Dane John Gardens, Canterbury
Map reference: Sheet 179; 147574
Access: Dane John stands in Public Gardens.

Canterbury's early history dates back at least as far as Dane John, a pre-Roman burial mound that the later Roman city wall deliberately goes round. At some stage it may have been heightened to provide a lookout, but it was never the keep of a Castle as many suggest. The nearby Canterbury Castle, built in 1080 (and one of the earliest stone keeps to survive in this country) obviated the need for an old fashioned Motte and Bailey construction.

  In 1790 Alderman James Simmonds decided to create a pleasure garden in that corner of the City and radically altered the appearance of the mound. He raised it to its present height, and shaped it to provide a 'belvedere' or viewing mound. A few years later a memorial vase was placed on the summit. The views of the City are not as good as they would have been in Alderman Simmond's day as he planted lime trees in the pleasure grounds, which have since matured, obscuring the view.

Places of Interest in the Neighbourhood
The Forgotten Port (Fordwich)
The Head was under the Bed (Canterbury)
Southern England's First Passenger Railway (Whitstable)

Dane John Mound, Canterbury which may be a burial mound.

75 The Fire on the Heath

Position: Penenden Heath, Maidstone
Map reference: Sheet 188; 775574
Access: Penenden Heath is a public Open Space.

The Penenden Heath that survives today is little more than a playing field and small area of sandy heathland, but it represents one of the most interesting parts of Kent, for it was traditionally the meeting place for residents of the county. It was the scene of trials, executions, rallies, riots and battles. The first recorded law suit in English history took place here in 1076, between Odo, Earl of Kent and Lanfranc, Archbishop of Canterbury.

Later events on the heath included the gathering of men in 1381 for the Peasants' Revolt, which then marched on London; the rebellion of 1554 against Queen Mary's marriage to Philip of Spain started here, as did the so called Battle of Maidstone in the Civil War.

Public executions took place on the Heath until 1830, the last man hanged here being John Dyke who was accused of setting a hay rick on fire. He was later buried in Bearsted Churchyard where a Canadian Cypress is said to mark the grave.

Meetings of the Shire Courts also took place on the Heath, the last of any significance being a petition presented in 1828 against the Catholic Emancipation Bill. It is recorded that 50,000 men attended, and that 'Kentish Fire' was heard. This is a peculiar type of clapping that was originally only to be found in Kent, but which has now been taken up by football fans worldwide. It consists of two slow claps followed by three short claps, and was originally used to signal agreement with the proceedings. 'Kentish Fire' is still to be heard at official functions in the county today.

Places of Interest in the Neighbourhood
The Sphinx of the West (Boxley)
A Trip to the Underworld (Maidstone)
The Volunteer's Memorial (Maidstone)

76 Where the Ball Drops on Time

Position: Deal Time Ball Tower
Map reference: Sheet 179; 379530
Access: The Time Ball Tower is open to the public at advertised times during the summer months.

The Time Ball Tower at Deal is a notable local landmark. It was originally built as a Semaphore Station late in the eighteenth century to ease communication between the town's Naval Dockyard and the Admiralty. The chain of such stations across the county can still be traced using an ordnance survey map and picking out names like 'Telegraph Hill'. It was said that messages could be transmitted from Deal to London in only two minutes, but it relied on operators using telescopes between each Station.

After the threat of a Napoleonic Invasion had passed the Semaphore Stations closed down. Many were converted to houses, or demolished, but the one at Deal survived, and in 1855 a time ball was installed on top of the tower. This time ball was raised to the top of its pole and dropped at exactly 1.00pm each day. There were also such balls at Greenwich, Falmouth, Portsmouth, Devonport, Portland, Southampton and Edinburgh. They provided shipping with an accurate time check, essential if they were to check their clocks before setting off on a long voyage.

The ball was dropped by electrical signal relayed via the South Eastern Railway lines from the Royal Observatory at Greenwich. There were elaborate instructions in case the ball failed to drop, or dropped at the wrong time, which included flying a flag. These contingency plans were brought into action on many occasions as teething problems were sorted out.

After years of neglect the Time Ball Tower was restored in 1988 and reopened as a Museum of Nautical Timekeeping. Its time ball now drops every hour for the benefit of visitors.

Places of Interest in the Neighbourhood
The Finest Eighteenth Century Ensemble (Waldershare)
Women, Officers and Soldiers (Dover)
Where the Romans got their Directions (Dover)

The Time Ball Tower was once a Semaphore Station.

77 Queen Anne's Bath House

Position: In the grounds of Lullingstone Castle
Map reference: Sheet 188; 531646
Access: Lullingstone Castle is open to the public at advertised times
during the summer months.

Lullingstone Castle is one of the least-known stately homes in the
county. It was built in the fifteenth century by Sir John Peche who
served in the Court of Henry VII, but was substantially altered by
subsequent owners. It is still the home of the descendants of the family
who built it. The most striking feature of the Castle is the splendid brick
gatehouse built in about 1497. There was formerly an inner gatehouse
too, but that has been demolished. The front of the Castle looks
eighteenth century, but this is the result of a re-facing, for once inside
the true age of the house becomes apparent.

In the early eighteenth century Percival Hart, owner of the Castle, was
a close friend of Queen Anne (1702-1714), a frequent visitor to the
Castle. Hart had always supported the Jacobite cause, and gloried in his

The ruins of Queen Anne's Bath House beside the River Darent.

close relationship with the Queen. In order that his house should be suitable to receive her he had it completely modernised, and the rooms the visitors see all bear the marks of his endeavours. New panelling was installed, a State Bed constructed, and a completely new staircase erected. Poor Queen Anne was extremely large (she had to be carried at her Coronation), so Percival Hart made his new staircase with deliberately shallow treads. Queen Anne was a High Church Anglican, very keen on church affairs, and the little church on the Castle lawn was also restored for her benefit, with a large porch and plaster ceiling.

Today the Castle contains many momentoes of her visits, including one of her childhood dolls, and a portrait possibly presented as a 'thank you' for the hospitality shown to her by Percival Hart.

The River Darent flows through the Park, and just across a bridge from the Castle stands a little ruined flint building constructed as a bath house for the exclusive use of Queen Anne. She was always suffering from poor health (not helped by her addiction to Brandy), and the therapeutic qualities of a little spring here were intended to help her health. Unfortunately the tiled interior has long since disappeared, as has the thatched roof.

Places of Interest in the Neighbourhood
Where the Rake made Little Progress (Bexley)
Where the Water Gushed Forth (Otford)
Lord Sackville's Birdhouse (Sevenoaks)

78 Margery the Martyr

Position: Pembury near Tunbridge Wells
Map reference: Sheet 188; 625407
Access: Margery Polley Memorial Trough stands on the village Green.

During the nineteenth century a large number of philanthropic works
were carried out by local landowners. A society for the establishment
of drinking fountains and cattle troughs was formed, and many were
placed at the tops of hills, or at busy cross roads. At Pembury a Mrs
Betts raised a subscription to erect a horse trough which would also
commemorate the martyrdom of Margery Polley, a local Protestant
during the reign of Queen Mary.

Margery Polley was a widow who refused to accept the Old Faith
re-introduced by Queen Mary after her accession in 1553. She eventually paid the inevitable price. In the summer of 1555 she was taken to
the Market Place in Tonbridge, where she was burned at the stake.
A fanciful engraving of the martyrdom was published in Foxe's *Book
of Martyrs.* It is possible that she was the first female martyr of the
Marian Persecutions, which claimed over 100 lives in the county.

There are other Martyr's memorials at Maidstone, Dartford,
Staplehurst and Canterbury.

Places of Interest in the Neighbourhood
The Hartlake Bridge Disaster (Hadlow)
Home of 'Disgusted' (Tunbridge Wells)
The Man who Attended his Own Funeral (Lamberhurst)

Margery Polley is remembered by this Horse Trough at Pembury.

79 The Pagan Altar in a Christian Church

Position: St Marys Church, Stone in Oxney
Map reference: Sheet 189; 940273
Access: The church stands on the hill overlooking Romney Marsh.

A great curiosity to those with an interest in the juxtaposition of objects is the Roman altar at Stone in Oxney Parish Church. Early Roman altars were constructed for Pagan Worship, and to find one in a medieval Kent church is a great surprise.

No one knows where the altar came from. It is possible that it originated at Lympne, along the edge of the Marsh, where there was a Roman Fort, but that does not explain how it found its way to this still remote area.

The altar is made of local ragstone and stands about 3 feet high and 2 feet square. It has the head of Mithras, the God of Roman Soldiers, carved on its sides, and a hollow in the top for offerings of oil and other gifts. It is first recorded in the area two hundred years ago when it stood by the Ferry. It may be that the iron ring now fixed into it dates from this time, for it was then used as a horse mounting block. At a later date it was placed in the church, as an object of antiquarian interest, although a later curate took a dislike to a pagan object being in his church and took it to the Vicarage garden. It was moved from there in 1926 to a place of safe keeping within the church where it has remained ever since.

Places of Interest in the Neighbourhood
The Largest Ditch in England (Appledore)
The Shocked Steeple (Brookland)
A Room with a View (Romney Marsh)

80 Off like a Rocket!

Position: Holy Trinity Church. Milton Regis
Map reference: Sheet 178; 909654
Access: The memorial can be seen in the churchyard.

One of the most unusual inscriptions in a Kent churchyard may be seen at the venerable old church of Milton Regis, just outside Sittingbourne. It records the strange, and sad, death of a churchwarden at the end of the seventeenth century.

> Here lyeth the
> body of Simon
> Gilker Junior
> who was killed by
> means of a rockett
> November 5th 1696
> Aged 48 Years

Whilst the details of the accident are not known it seems from the date that this accident was caused at a celebration of Guy Fawkes Night, less than a hundred years after the Gunpowder Plot. We know that a commemoration of the events of 1605 were held in most towns, and that they were not the jocular events we know today, being based to a far greater extent on anti-Papal demonstrations. So it would not be surprising to find a churchwarden taking an active part in the organisation of such an occasion. The use of rockets was popular, especially in this part of Kent where people had access to two sorts of explosive.

The Naval Dockyards in the area, at Chatham and Sheerness, must have used warning rockets, and it has been suggested that some of these were used each November 5th. Similarly, the Gunpowder Works at Faversham were well established by the late seventeenth century, and possibly some sort of home-made rockets were employed here at Sittingbourne – with fatal consequences.

Places of Interest in the Neighbourhood
An Englishman Abroad (Gillingham)
The Ship on the Shore (Minster in Sheppey)
Where Wellington got his Powder

Simon Gilker's gravestone in Milton Regis Churchyard.

Index

Places by page number

The Curiosities of England

The following titles in the series have already been published and can be ordered at all bookshops, or in case of difficulties direct from the publishers.